ONLINE LEARNING AND TEACHING WITH TECHNOLOGY

ONLINE LEARNING AND TEACHING WITH TECHNOLOGY

CASE STUDIES, EXPERIENCE AND PRACTICE

EDITED BY
DAVID MURPHY, ROB WALKER
AND GRAHAM WEBB

CASE STUDIES OF TEACHING IN HIGHER EDUCATION

KOGAN PAGE

First published in 2001

Kogan Page Limited
120 Pentonville Road
London N1 9JN
UK

Stylus Publishing Inc.
22883 Quicksilver Drive
Sterling VA 20166–2012
USA

British Library Cataloguing in Publication Data

A CIP record for this book is available from the British Library.

ISBN 0 7494 3520 8 (paperback)
ISBN 0 7494 3529 1 (hardback)

Typeset by Saxon Graphics Ltd, Derby
Printed and bound in Great Britain by Biddles Ltd, Guildford and King's Lynn

Contents

Contributors   *viii*

Introduction   1

THE CASE STUDIES

Section 1: Student Interaction Issues

1. **Flame War** *Mike Robertshaw*   13
   Calming the protagonists in a flame war; facing the consequences
   of action taken
2. **Do Students Really Want to Interact?** *Lori Wallace*   21
   Working over a period of time to encourage distance education
   students to interact, using a variety of technologies
3. **Pacific Mayday: Conviviality Overboard** *Roger Boshier*   28
   Finding a surprising amount of antagonism between students from
   seemingly similar contexts
4. **Do We Really Need an Online Discussion Group?** *Charlotte*   36
   Gunawardena, Jan Plass and Mark Salisbury
   Designing an interactive online environment and discovering that
   the students don't use it
5. **Houston, We Have a Problem!** *Catherine McLoughlin and*
   Joe Luca   44
   Dealing with problems encountered by groups of students
   working in teams in an online environment

Section 2: Teaching and Assessment Issues

6. **Teaching Online... Reluctantly** *Bob Fox*   55
   Becoming reluctantly involved in online delivery and subsequently
   being perceived as a leader in the use of the technology

7. **Try, Try Again!** *Stephanie Tarbin and Chris Trevitt*   63
   Overcoming student resistance to new methods of learning,
   involving the introduction of an online discussion group
8. **Credit Where It's Due** *Robin Goodfellow*   73
   Creating an equitable assessment system for group work in an
   international online course
9. **It Seemed Like a Good Idea at the Time** *Ron Oliver*   81
   Introducing innovative tasks for students working online and
   encountering negative reactions

Section 3: Planning and Development Issues

10. **Of Heaven and Hell** *Leonie Rowan and Chris Bigum*   91
    Using scenario planning to map out an approach to teaching with
    videoconference technology
11. **From Mouldy Disks to Online Fix** *Vikki Ravaga,*   99
    Jennifer Evans, Taaloga Faasalaina and Jo Osborne
    Facing the pressures of teaching computing to a widely dispersed
    group of students with inadequate access to the required
    technology
12. **'I Have Some Pages Up!'** *Jo Bruce and Ruth Goodall*   107
    Working 'one-to-one' to assist academic staff to create their own
    subject Web sites
13. **The Reluctant Software Developers** *Leonard Webster and*   114
    David Murphy
    Developing a software tool to encourage collaboration and
    interaction in an online environment
14. **The Great Courseware Gamble** *Bridget Somekh*   121
    The trials and tribulations of a government-funded courseware
    development project
15. **Poetic Seeing** *Lee Kar Tin and Wong Lai Fong*   129
    Implementing curriculum reform through the development of
    multimedia

Section 4: Policy Issues

16. **Who is Leading Whom?** *Michelle Selinger*   139
    Developing appropriate skills in information and communication
    technologies while simultaneously satisfying governmental
    statutory requirements

17. **Travelling Without Maps** *Alison Littler and Jan Mahyuddin*   146
    Creating resource materials to support editing staff in upgrading
    their skills in online development

18. **Techno Hero Fiasco** *Julianne Moss, Mary Fearnley-Sander*   155
     and Claire Hiller
     Coping with the pressures of creating new and innovative learning
     environments in a short timescale; suffering the consequences of
     failing technology
19. **The Tragedy of the Early Adopters** *Mark Smithers and*   162
     Christine Spratt
     Taking the lead in technological advancement; coping with the
     effects of isolation and rejection of peers

Conclusion   171

Further Reading   175

Index   177

CONTRIBUTORS

Chris Bigum is Associate Professor and Associate Dean (Research) in the Faculty of Education and Creative Arts at the University of Central Queensland, Rockhampton, Australia (e-mail: bigumc@cqu.edu.au)

Roger Boshier is Professor of Adult Education at the University of British Columbia, Vancouver, Canada (e-mail: Roger.Boshier@ubc.ca)

Jo Bruce is a Web officer at the University of East Anglia, UK (e-mail: joanne.bruce@uea.ac.uk)

Jennifer Evans is an editor of distance education materials at the University of the South Pacific, Fiji (e-mail: evans_j@usp.ac.fj)

Taaloga Faasalaina is an instructional designer now working at the University of the South Pacific's campus in Samoa (e-mail: faasalaina_t@samoa.usp.ac.fj)

Mary Fearnley-Sander is Lecturer in the School of Secondary and Post-compulsory Education at the University of Tasmania, Hobart, Australia (e-mail: Mary.FearnleySander@utas.edu.au)

Bob Fox is Associate Professor in the Centre for IT in School and Teacher Education at the University of Hong Kong (e-mail: foxrmk@hkucc.hku.hk)

Ruth Goodall is Director of the Centre for Staff and Educational Development at the University of East Anglia, UK (e-mail: r.e.goodall@uea.ac.uk)

Robin Goodfellow is Head of the Centre for Information Technology in Education at the Open University's Institute of Educational Technology in Milton Keynes, UK (e-mail: R.Goodfellow@open.ac.uk)

Charlotte Gunawardena is Associate Professor at the University of New Mexico, USA (e-mail: lani@unm.edu)

Claire Hiller is Senior Lecturer in the School of Secondary and Post-compulsory Education at the University of Tasmania, Hobart, Australia (e-mail: Claire.Hiller@utas.edu.au)

Lee Kar Tin is Head of the Department of Curriculum and Instruction at the Hong Kong Institute of Education (e-mail: ktlee@ied.edu.hk)

Wong Lai Fong is Lecturer in the Department of Creative Arts, Hong Kong Institute of Education (e-mail: lfwong@ied.edu.hk)

Alison Littler is a program developer at the Open University, Milton Keynes, UK (e-mail: A.D.Littler@open.ac.uk)

Joe Luca is Lecturer in the School of Communications and Multimedia at Edith Cowan University, Perth, Australia (e-mail: j.luca@metz.une.edu.au)

Catherine McLoughlin is Senior Lecturer in Higher Education at the University of New England, Armidale, Australia (e-mail: mcloughlin@metz.une.edu.au)

Jan Mahyuddin is an editor at Deakin University, Geelong, Australia (e-mail: janmah@deakin.edu.au)

Julianne Moss is Lecturer in Early Childhood and Primary Education at the University of Tasmania, Hobart, Australia (e-mail: Julianne.Moss@utas.edu.au)

David Murphy is Associate Professor in the Educational Technology and Publishing Unit at the Open University of Hong Kong (e-mail: dmurphy@ouhk.edu.hk)

Ron Oliver is Associate Professor in the School of Communications and Multimedia at Edith Cowan University, Perth, Australia (e-mail: r.oliver@cowan.edu.au)

Jo Osborne is currently Acting Head of Distance Education at the University of the South Pacific, Fiji (e-mail: osborne_je@usp.ac.fj)

Jan Plass is Assistant Professor at New York University, USA (e-mail: jan.plass@nyu.edu)

Vikki Ravaga is an instructional designer, previously of the University of the South Pacific, Fiji, but now at the Central West College of TAFE, Geraldton, Western Australia (e-mail: ravaga_v@centralwest.wa.gov.au)

Mike Robertshaw is Associate Professor in the School of Science and Technology at the Open University of Hong Kong (e-mail: mrobert@ouhk.edu.hk)

Leonie Rowan is Senior Lecturer in the Faculty of Education and Creative Arts at the University of Central Queensland, Rockhampton, Australia (e-mail: l.rowan@cqu.edu.au)

Mark Salisbury is Assistant Professor at the University of New Mexico, USA (e-mail: salisbu@unm.edu)

Mark Smithers is Web Manager and Lead Developer at Commander Communications Ltd (e-mail: msmithers@commander.com.au)

Michelle Selinger is an Educational Specialist at CISCO Systems (e-mail: m.s.selinger@warwick.ac.uk)

Bridget Somekh is Professor of Education at Manchester Metropolitan University, UK (e-mail: b.somekh@mmu.ac.uk)

Christine Spratt is Director of Teaching and Learning in the Faculty of Health Science at the University of Tasmania (e-mail: Christine.Spratt@utas.edu.au)

Stephanie Tarbin is Lecturer at the Australian National University, Canberra, Australia (e-mail: Stephanie.Tarbin@anu.edu.au)

Chris Trevitt is Senior Lecturer at the Australian National University, Canberra, Australia (e-mail: Chris.Trevitt@anu.edu.au)

Rob Walker is Senior Lecturer in the Centre for Applied Research in Education at the University of East Anglia, UK (e-mail: Rob.Walker@uea.ac.uk)

Lori Wallace is Director of the Distance Education Program at the University of Manitoba, Winnipeg, Canada (e-mail: L_wallace@umanitoba.ca)

Graham Webb is Professor and Director, Centre for Higher Education Quality at Monash University, Melbourne, Australia (e-mail: graham.webb@adm.monash.edu.au)

Leonard Webster is Director of Educational Development and Flexible Learning in the Faculty of Law at Monash University, Melbourne, Australia (e-mail: len.webster@law.monash.edu.au)

INTRODUCTION

Of all the blue-sky scenarios and vapourware solutions offered by those who promote information technology, online learning has become the most pressing and pervasive. As thousands of academics, millions of students, as well as librarians, support staff and administrators struggle daily to come to terms with its actual strengths, weaknesses and idiosyncrasies, the promises of the Internet continue to develop unabated. With every special newspaper supplement, it seems, those in the business offer new visions, new services we didn't know we needed, yet more exciting equipment and software possibilities that lie just over the horizon and, less well-publicized, an increasing number of routes to what may be educational dead ends.

This book charts the struggles of tertiary teachers as they attempt to harness technology and to realize its positive potential. As they tell their stories it is important to remember that their efforts to innovate are more often than not conducted against a background of managing with decreased resources, increased teaching loads, short-term contracts and the twin demands of quality assurance and increased expectations. Their accounts offer an insight to the challenges they have faced and sometimes, but not always, conquered. Their experiences may help others to avoid the pitfalls and problems that can beset 'early adopters'. Perhaps not surprisingly, though the technologies are new, the narratives told by the early adopters are often surprisingly familiar.

Whether or not you have yet taken part in the headlong rush into online learning, you have doubtless encountered examples of online courses: some good, many bad and most requiring too much on-screen reading (Boshier *et al*, 1997). This book is not designed to teach you how to put your course online as there are plenty of existing practical texts designed for this purpose (Horton, 2000; Palloff and Pratt, 1999) as well as others with an emphasis on educational issues and concerns (Abbey, 2000). Rather, this collection of case studies offers a variety of experiences from those who have moved towards online learning and have been willing to put their educational ideas to the test in this challenging and tantalizingly promising medium.

TEACHING AND LEARNING WITH TECHNOLOGY

With anything that looks new, it is important to remember that most things remain the same. We start from the (somewhat contentious) view that all teaching involves technology. Given a broad view of technology, that it comprises tools that extend human perception and human action and the assumption that all human communication is in some way mediated, then it is clear that what we take as conventional teaching involves some form of technology and some degree of mediation. And while the technology itself may have changed, it is still a technology with a history.

In this view, the classroom itself is a technology, or comprises a set of technologies which we mostly take for granted – physical materials such as desks and chairs, black, white and green boards, chalk, pens, projection devices, worksheets, textbooks, notebooks, lighting and sound regimes and so on. It also includes the social practices we have developed to manage these tools and settings: lectures, group activities, labs and field trips, for example. Technologically enhanced teaching and learning, in this view, is not new.

While this might sound pedantic, the shift in thinking from the view that technology is new and will revolutionize teaching, to seeing it as but another step in a long sequence of changes, helps us to better understand the problem. Even if we restrict ourselves to inventions that 'technologize' environments in a narrower sense, then these have been with us for a long time too, and have a chequered history. The story of educational innovation is littered with the remains of seemingly revolutionary gadgets and systems (remember the 'teaching machine'?), machines that have changed their function (the telephone) and others that have quietly infiltrated and become part-and-parcel of the educational landscape (the photocopier and the OHP). Some technologies, such as educational television, have generally not lived up to the initial promise propounded by their early champions, but nevertheless have settled down to become accepted as 'part of the furniture' in many educational programmes.

But despite the lessons of history, there has been a rush by individual academics and even more by institutions, to become involved in online education. Information Technology (IT) has infiltrated not just practice but policy in a way that no other teaching technology has done in the past. Governments, in particular, have seized on IT as a device for 'modernizing' education, and institutions have vied with one another to stand in the front line. As with so many other technologies (as varied as open-plan building design, strip lighting, staff appraisal, the spreadsheet, Windows environments, management by objectives, quality assurance) what has been developed by the business sector has been sold on to education with the line that it is not just new, but effective and efficient.

In this book we are concerned with practice rather than with image. We take a wide view of what constitutes online learning, including a course that is essentially face to face but is supplemented by resources located on a Web site, through to wholly online courses for which all content materials, activities, assessment and communication are provided via the Internet. We find that the most pressing concerns are about learning activities, assessment and communication (especially interaction via online discussion groups) and these constitute the bulk of the topics raised in the case studies in this book.

THE CASE STUDIES

We began with a broad view of technology and in our initial approach to authors for the case studies we did not tightly specify which particular technology should provide the focus. However, almost universally, the authors chose their case studies from their experiences with various forms of online learning. Even those that did not do so perceive that the next stage of their technological development will be with online technologies. Thus, as the case studies emerged, the focus of the book moved towards the struggles, successes and failures of faculty in teaching online.

The 19 cases are written by 34 faculty members from Australia, Canada, Hong Kong, the Pacific, the UK and the United States. They come from a range of disciplines and backgrounds including adult education, art education, building studies, business studies, computing, distance education, education development, history, IT, instructional systems development, staff development and teacher education. Contributors were invited to tell the story of a critical incident that has actually happened to them, and which led to them learning and growing in their journey as teachers using technology. Each case study tells a real story based on an actual situation and its resolution.

As with previous books in this series (see Edwards, Smith and Webb, 2001; Schwartz, Mennin and Web, 2001), each case study is preceded by an indication of the main issue or issues raised, and by brief background information to set the context for the 'action'.

We did not predetermine the issues and in fact many of them were identified only after we had the case account. We think this is important. One of the recurring problems that emerges in the educational use of technologies is that the technology is given pole position. The user is then placed in the position of adapting to the demands (or functionalities) of the technology. The technology becomes the leading actor. We were anxious not to reinforce this pattern, so we asked writers to tell us their stories first, and to identify the key issues only when this was done.

The case study proper consists of two or more parts, each concluding with a few questions for you, the reader, to consider. We have introduced this reflective break between parts of a case study at a point where an action must be taken and/or a decision made. You are invited to step into the writer's shoes at this point and decide not only what you think *should* be done next but also what you think *will actually happen* next given the circumstances. After discovering what actually *did* happen, you will be asked to reflect on how the situation was handled and to consider some of the questions and issues raised by the case study. At the end there is a case reporter's discussion that raises questions such as:

- How well was the situation handled?
- What other options might there have been for dealing with it?
- What lessons did the reporter and his or her colleagues learn from the experience?
- What lessons are there for others from the case?

The discussions are by no means exhaustive in that other important issues and/or questions could be examined, and you may well identify issues or perspectives that have not been mentioned. We sought to strike a balance between leaving each situation equivocal and open to individual interpretation on the one hand and tightly defining issues and providing guidance on the other. Nor is the discussion intended to give 'the right answer' to a problem. We do not believe that there is a simple and unequivocal 'right answer' in cases such as these, although, under the circumstances described, some solutions may be better than others. The purpose of the discussion is to explore the issues raised and to encourage you to make your own decisions based upon your interpretation of and reflections on the case. The intention is that you may then apply the insights gained from this experience as you deal with similar situations in your own efforts to teach online.

The book concludes with a brief list of suggested readings on teaching with technology. Most of them are of general applicability rather than being directed toward specific issues or events discussed in the case studies. The reading list is intended to be broad and immediately useful, rather than comprehensive. The editors and contributors would welcome enquiries from readers who would like more information. E-mail addresses are given for the editors and for case reporters.

ISSUES IN ONLINE LEARNING AND TEACHING WITH TECHNOLOGY

As the case studies in this book developed, a number of issues about teaching with technology, in particular teaching online, emerged. Further, although many of the case studies involved more than one issue, they were reasonably easily placed in one of the four key areas.

One of the great attractions of online learning has been, not just in terms of its improved efficiency and effectiveness, but in the promise it offers to open up access to aspects of the academy that have previously been hidden or beyond reach. In particular, many claim that what is most important educationally in the new media is its increased capacity to support 'interaction'. This is a problematic concept, but nevertheless, the capacity of IT to foster and support increased *student interaction* is seen by many commentators as crucial.

Harasim (1989) describes the part that online interaction can play in collaborative learning environments, emphasizing the positive effects of being actively engaged in learning, including sharing information and perspectives through interaction with other learners. This form of communication can, it is claimed, promote reflective thinking, and offers increased flexibility of time and place of learning (eg Bates, 1995; Harasim *et al*, 1995). As well as allowing flexibility, online discussion groups can help to reduce the isolation of learning at a distance, and play an important role in the social aspects of learning (Harasim *et al*, 1995; Mason and Weller, 2000).

Interaction emerges as a key issue in the case studies presented here, and has been taken up in a variety of ways. In some cases, carefully constructed interactive environments have resulted in disappointingly low levels of interactivity. Others have taken off, only to lead to tension, argument and discord. The ways in which faculty have reacted to such incidents are documented in a number of case studies concerning this issue. Given its immediacy and relevance to all those facing the prospect of teaching online or already doing so, the case studies focused on this issue are presented first.

The case studies also reveal how faculty have coped with the *teaching and assessment* issues that arise when involved in online learning (Bennett, Priest and Macpherson, 1999; Carr-Chellman and Duschatel, 2000; Salmon, 2000). This includes not just the early adopters of technology, but those more traditional teachers who find themselves caught up in the rush towards online learning, and who on occasion find it much more satisfying and rewarding than anticipated.

Teaching online has presented challenges to those involved in the *planning and development* of educational environments that rely on technology (Laurillard, 1993; Oliver, 2000), and these challenges constitute another of the issues about which the writers have presented case studies. For while each of the cases described here has its focus on the intimacies of learning and teaching, organizational and policy issues often follow close behind. The rapid change in type and availability of technologies to both faculty and students has meant that planning and development have to take place on 'shifting sands' that threaten to make commitment to particular software or hardware a hazardous occupation. It has also led to the need for staff development, not just for faculty, but also for other staff and, of course, the students.

Then there is the issue of *policy-led* technological development (Bates,

2000). Universities everywhere have been faced with the pressure to 'go online' and some have responded by introducing policies and strategies to guide development. Some of the case study writers have told of how they have developed online learning materials 'by decree'. The inevitable short-comings and failures that have resulted are handled in a variety of ways, in all cases having significant impact on those teaching online. Other writers have found their pioneering efforts to lead the way within their organization thwarted as the university introduces a standardized solution or software package to be used for all online development.

HOW TO USE THIS BOOK

We recommend that, as you read each case study, you 'play the game' and read only Part 1, before reflecting and noting your impressions of what is going on, what courses of action could be taken next, what you think *will* happen next and what course of action *you* would pursue. The same applies to Part 2 (and others, where relevant). Questions have been provided at the end of each part of a case study to assist you in framing your interpretation of and response to what is happening. In many instances, the questions are specific to the case, but some general questions that would be appropriate for most cases include the following.

At the end of Part 1, ask:

- What is going on here?
- What factors may have contributed to the situation described?
- How does the case reporter appear to see the situation?
- What *other* interpretations might there be?
- Where are there obvious gaps and silences in the story?
- Are some aspects of the case more predictable than others?
- What evidence might you need to think out how the scenario might develop?
- How might those in it handle the situation best?
- What sorts of consequences might be expected from the possible actions?
- Given the nature of the participants, how will the situation probably be dealt with?

After the final part and the discussion, ask:

- How was the situation handled?
- What general issues are brought out by the case?
- What do the case and its issues mean for you, the reader?

We believe that as an individual reader you will derive valuable insights if you use the case studies and discussions in this way. However, we suggest that you will also find it valuable to meet with colleagues to share impressions of the cases and insights obtained from them. The case studies can serve as resources for advanced training and development of teaching staff and administrators. In fact, the case studies presented in Schwartz and Webb (1993) were both the products of, and the discussion materials for, a series of group discussions in a faculty development programme. Others have also described the use of case studies in faculty development for teachers (Christensen, 1987; Hutchings, 1993; Wilkerson and Boehrer, 1992). Those coming to the case studies from an education or social science background may also recognize them as 'case accounts' or 'case methods' (Shulman, 1992) rather than case studies as defined by Stake (1994; 1995) and Yin (1994).

Whether done formally or informally, consideration of the case studies and issues by groups of colleagues has benefits beyond those that may be obtained from individual reading. In discussions with colleagues, faculty involved with online teaching can confront their own perceptions and readings and face the possibility that others may not share their interpretations. Justifying these interpretations can bring teachers face to face with their philosophies of human nature and the nature of education. This can serve to stimulate them to become more reflective about their own practices. They may be challenged to come to terms with alternative conceptions and interpretations of each case. Teachers may be stimulated to re-examine and re-evaluate some of the central features of their own views by seeking to understand one another's interpretations and experiences and the outlooks that shape them. The discussion sections in this book may provide a starting point, but there are further opportunities for quality discussion between colleagues on these issues.

Reflection in teaching is crucial regardless of whether you read the cases as an individual or discuss them with colleagues. It is from this effort that teachers are likely to obtain the most benefit from the cases (Fincher *et al*, 2000; Harden *et al*, 1999). Interestingly, the case study writers themselves, in developing the cases for this book, discovered the value of reflecting on the educational experiences they reported. They had the courage to openly discuss some critical experiences and in doing so they have identified issues you can continue to reflect on and explore since there are clearly no quick fixes to the issues raised.

We trust that your own reflection on teaching with technology and on the issues raised by the case studies presented in this book will be useful and will stimulate you to try new approaches in your own teaching in order to make appropriate use of new and emerging technologies. We wish you (and your students!) every success.

References

Abbey, B (ed) (2000) *Instructional and Cognitive Impacts of Web-based Education*, Idea Group Publishing, Hershey, USA

Bates, A W (1995) *Technology, Open Learning and Distance Education*, Routledge, London

Bates, A W (2000) *Managing Technological Change: Strategies for college and university leaders*, Jossey-Bass, Windsor, Ontario

Bennett, S, Priest, A-M and Macpherson, C (1999) 'Learning about online learning: An approach to staff development for university teachers', *Australian Journal of Educational Technology*, **15**, 3, pp 207–21

Boshier, R, Mohapi, M, Moulton, G, Qayyum, A, Sadownik, L and Wilson, M (1997) 'Best and worst dressed web courses: Strutting into the 21st century in comfort and style', *Distance Education*, **18**, 2, pp 327–48

Carr-Chellman, A and Duschatel, P (2000) 'The ideal online course', *British Journal of Educational Technology*, **31**, 3, pp 229–41

Christensen, C R (1987) *Teaching and the Case Method*, Harvard Business School, Boston, MA

Edwards, H, Smith, B and Webb, G (2001) *Lecturing: Case studies, experience and practice*, Kogan Page, London

Fincher, R-M, Simpson, D E, Mennin, S P, Rosenfeld, G C, Rothman, A, Cole McGrew, M, Hansen, P A, Mazmanian, P E and Turnbull, J M (2000) 'Scholarship in teaching: an imperative for the 21st century', *Academic Medicine*, **75** pp 887–94

Harasim, L (1989) 'Online education: A new domain', in R Mason and A Kaye (eds), *Mindweave: Communication, computers and distance education*, pp 50–57, Pergamon Press, Oxford

Harasim, L, Hiltz, S R, Teles, L and Turoff, M (1995) *Learning Networks: A field guide to teaching and learning on-line*, The MIT Press, Cambridge, MA

Harden, R M, Grant, J, Buckley, G and Hart, I R (1999) 'BEME Guide No. 1: Best evidence medical education', *Medical Teacher*, **21**, pp 553–62

Horton, W (2000) *Designing Web-based Training*, Wiley, New York

Hutchings, P (1993) *Using Cases to Improve College Teaching: A guide to more reflective practice*, American Association for Higher Education, Washington, DC

Laurillard, D (1993) *Rethinking University Teaching: A framework for the effective use of educational technology*, Routledge, London

Mason, R and Weller, M (2000) 'Factors affecting students' satisfaction on a web course', *Australian Journal of Educational Technology*, **16**, 2, pp 173–200

Oliver, R (2000) 'When teaching meets learning: design principles and strategies for web-based learning environments that support knowledge construction', in R Sims, M O'Reilly and S Sawkins (eds), *Learning to Choose: Choosing to learn*, Proceedings of the 17th Annual ASCILITE Conference, Southern Cross University Press, Lismore, NSW

Palloff, R and Pratt, K (1999) *Building Learning Communities in Cyberspace: Effective strategies for the online classroom*, Jossey Bass, San Francisco, CA

Salmon, G (2000) *E-moderating: The key to teaching and learning online*, Kogan Page, London

Schwartz, P and Webb, G (1993) *Case Studies on Teaching in Higher Education*, Kogan Page, London

Schwartz, P, Mennin, S and Webb, G (2001) *Problem-Based Learning: Case studies, experience and practice*, Kogan Page, London

Shulman, J H (ed) (1992) *Case Methods in Teacher Education*, Teachers College Press, Columbia University, New York

Stake, R E (1994) 'Case study', in N Denzin and Y Lincoln (eds), *Handbook of Qualitative Research,* pp 236–47, Sage, Thousand Oaks, CA

Stake, R E (1995) *The Art of Case Study Research*, Sage, Thousand Oaks, CA

Wilkerson, L and Boehrer, J (1992) 'Using cases about teaching for faculty development', *To Improve the Academy,* **11**, pp 253–62

Yin, R (1994) *Case Study Research: Design and methods*, Sage, Newbury Park, CA

SECTION 1

STUDENT INTERACTION ISSUES

CHAPTER 1

FLAME WAR

Case reporter: Mike Robertshaw

Issues raised

The issue raised by this case study is conflict in an online environment (flame war). Particular issues include whether it is appropriate to manipulate student conflict to meet course aims, and what is the most effective means of resolving online conflict.

Background

U123 is a distance education course that teaches about the Internet to around 150 off-campus students in Hong Kong. Nearly all students use English as their second language and students are working adults studying part time. As an introductory course newly added to the university's curriculum it attracts a diverse collection of students from a variety of disciplines and backgrounds. Both sexes are well represented in each presentation. Mike, the course developer and coordinator, had worked in distance education for over 10 years. While his area of specialization is maths his interests have grown to include the Internet generally and its uses in distance education in particular. Course content is provided mostly in hard copy units although some is presented through the course Web site. All other communication, including course-related activities, is via the Internet. The course has unmoderated newsgroups for course-related activities such as debates and announcements, as well as for non-course related advice.

PART 1

I was delighted at the apparent success of my experiment in facilitating inter-action in a distance education environment. Use of the Internet had given students easy access to one another for the first time. Students were beginning to form communities and develop a sense of belonging that is difficult to create with individuals who usually only meet in face-to-face tuto-rials every five to six weeks.

After an initial period for test messages, students were informed by e-mail that, to avoid excessive 'noise', they must only send messages to the mailing list that directly related to one of the official debates or to a topic sanctioned by the lecturer. Students were instructed that other messages should instead go to the appropriate newsgroup. The code of conduct (published in the course guide and on the course Web site) included the statement: 'Treat others as you would like to be treated.'

Early in the course a small group of students attempted to establish a student Internet Association (IA) and I agreed that they could post messages to the mailing list to publicize meetings and minutes. This decision was communicated to students at the beginning of the course and in the first three months of the course the IA sent half a dozen messages.

During this period, however, other students did not pay attention to the instructions about using the list and there were regular complaints to the list about this behaviour! I had opted to censure offending students through direct e-mail rather than through the list, although regular reminders about the expected behaviour were sent to the list.

The following exchange started during a weekend (the names here being student 'nicknames', which preserved the anonymity of participants – the students did not know with whom they were interacting). Following one IA message to the list posted during the weekend a student named Tony replied with a strongly worded complaint about the IA messages, which he saw as 'repetitive abuse [of] this mailing list'. Mary, one of the IA students, replied to Tony on the list explaining that permission for IA to use the list had been obtained and objecting to the tone of his message. Tony misinterpreted Mary's reply by reading it as a personal rebuke rather than a simple statement of fact and an expression of opinion. This was a classic example of the reader of an e-mail injecting tone into the text that didn't appear to be justified from the content. Tony rejected her explanation in a message to the list using 'shameful' to describe Mary's actions.

At this point John joined in to try to placate Tony through the list while at the same time indicating that Tony had overreacted. Tony interpreted this as an attack and an attempt to get him to shut up. Tony rebutted John's comments and accused him of arguing against free speech. John and several other students then counterattacked by pointing out that Tony was now himself misusing the list. On the Monday morning I discovered that war, or 'flame war' as it is called on the Internet, was in full swing, with about 30 messages sent to the list mostly directed at Tony. Most of the messages were very long and aggressive. In addition, I had a number of e-mails sent directly to me complaining about the general abuse of the mailing list plus one from Mary who had clearly been upset by the public attack on her. What should I do?

What do you think were the main reasons for the development of the flame war?
Could anything have been done differently to prevent it from happening?
What do you think the teacher will do?
If you were in this situation, what would you do next?

PART 2

I replied to the direct e-mail messages indicating that I was aware of what was happening and sympathizing with Mary, but pointing out how easy it was for e-mails to be misinterpreted. As part of the course is concerned with 'netiquette' and flame wars I was tempted to take this opportunity to let students experience how such exchanges can grow out of control. In addition, students were for the first time publicly demonstrating passion and willingness to challenge another's opinions. I gave into temptation and allowed the exchange on the list to continue without any direct interference from me on the mailing list or any attempt to calm the participants. I hoped that the flame war would demonstrate to students the need to be careful in preparing e-mail messages to be sent to a public forum.

The pace of the war increased as each new attempt by a student to placate either or both parties resulted in a new attack, and so the war widened.

By mid-week the flame war appeared to be dying down in the discussion group, mainly because Tony had changed his form of attack. He 'mailbombed' two of the students, including John. This involves sending many long messages containing gibberish to the students' accounts. These filled their accounts and prevented any other messages from being received until the messages had been downloaded and deleted – a time-consuming task. Tony had attempted to make his latest attack anonymous, but John had sufficient technical expertise to be able to trace the attack back to Tony.

John e-mailed me, complaining about Tony and demanding action. At this point I decided that the attacks had gone too far and intervened directly. I e-mailed the list reminding students of my decision to allow IA to use the list, reminding them of the rules for using the list and requesting any further discussion to continue in the general newsgroup, if at all. I also e-mailed Tony directly asking him to stop 'mailbombing' students and to stop sending messages to the list that did not relate to the debates.

Tony refused to cooperate and on the list accused me of taking sides. He argued that he had the right to use the list to defend himself in the face of personal attacks. I reassured him in a direct e-mail message that I was not taking sides, but that he and the others were all guilty of misusing the list. Our exchange continued with his messages appearing on the list and my replies going to him directly. In the meantime the original flame war on the list restarted with the other students condemning Tony for the 'mail-bombing' and for attacking me. I e-mailed each student directly, indicating that the best way of stopping the flame war was for students not to respond to Tony's messages.

By this time I was convinced that Tony was enjoying being the centre of attention. I was receiving more direct complaints from students about the noise on the list and about my apparent failure to respond publicly. Several students expressed concern about participating in the course debates, as they feared becoming the subject of a flame war themselves. Certainly, most students' contributions to the debates became relatively non-controversial and participation in the current debate fell rapidly. In fact, the flame war had become so bad that I had to delay the introduction of the next subject for debate as I felt that students would not be willing to join in given the current atmosphere.

What would you do at this stage?
How does this Internet-based conflict differ from conflicts between students in face-to-face environments?
Do lecturers need to be seen by all students to be publicly censuring 'unruly' students?

PART 3

It had become clear that Tony was not going to stop using the list to attack other individuals on the course and that the mailing list was in danger of losing its effectiveness as a means of debate. Through the different mailing lists on online education I had read of similar situations in which conflicts has arisen in course-related Internet channels. I found most of the discussions difficult to relate to as nearly all involved comparatively small numbers of US students within a culture very different to that in Hong Kong. I was reluctant to post my own problem for advice – perhaps from a sense of guilt that I'd deliberately let the situation develop to its current level. Certainly my experience in an on-campus environment was not particularly helpful. In a face-to-face situation it usually only took my presence to calm students to the point where at least the 'shouting' stopped.

I checked with the Registrar as to what action, if any, could be taken by the university if Tony continued his activities. The administration admitted that it had not considered this type of scenario and had no immediate strategy. I found myself having to search through the existing regulations for some means through which I could apply pressure to anyone who refused to end the flame war. As the use of the Internet in courses is not specifically addressed in regulations we finally decided that if necessary the regulation forbidding any student from hindering the study of another student could be applied, particularly if the 'mailbombing' continued.

In determining how to proceed I felt that there was a need to place the events into context with all of the students, as much of the passion had arisen from messages written in haste and under the protection of electronic anonymity. For Tony I decided that since reason was apparently not working and my direct involvement was not calming him down it was time to use the threat of disciplinary action; however, this threat should not be directed only at him since, although he was the main, he was not the only protagonist.

I sent a message reminding everyone how easy it was to misinterpret e-mail messages written in haste and how the machine interface can sometimes change an individual's behaviour. I also explained that intentionally disrupting study could be interpreted as a disciplinary offence and that the flame war and 'mailbombing' had disrupted the smooth presentation of the course.

It had the desired effect on the students as a whole – the tone of messages improved and the flame war ended. Tony stopped his aggressive behaviour but later withdrew from the course without ever making another contribution to any of the communication channels.

In the end-of-course feedback many students referred to the flame war as making them realize the importance of carefully wording messages to public forums on the Internet and of not jumping to conclusions about any malicious intent in messages from others. Some students commented that the flame war had been the only really interesting student exchange during the course! Many students, however, admitted that they had found the public attacks on individuals so intimidating that they were now reluctant to participate in public Internet exchanges.

How well was the situation handled?
Would you have handled the situation differently?
What are the implications for your own teaching that can be taken from this case?

CASE REPORTER'S DISCUSSION

The case concerns my attempt to encourage students to engage in open debate – an activity most would consider to lie at the core of undergraduate learning. I wanted to provide students with the means to interact with each other that they would otherwise miss in a distance education environment where students rarely meet face to face. By not intervening in a series of angry online exchanges between students I was not only able to provide them with direct experience of part of the course, but was also able to encourage them to abandon their reluctance to challenge others publicly.

The account raises a number of issues that most academics will face at some time:

- Was this major disturbance to the educational environment justified (in that it provided a demonstration of one topic and also overcame the passive nature of students)?
- Does the use of Internet technology introduce any unique features into such conflicts?
- What form should a teacher's intervention take in a virtual conflict?

Debate between students is clearly a justifiable aim in any course. When students challenge each other's perceptions, individuals often realize the real strengths or weaknesses of their own beliefs or understanding. It is also inevitable that some exchanges may get heated; however, lecturers should only deliberately promote passionate debate when they know how to control it quickly before tempers are lost and 'fists fly'. Certainly the situation should not be allowed to interfere with the smooth, planned presentation of the course. Neither should matters be allowed to deteriorate to the point where students are engaging in personal attacks rather than academic debate. One of the 'rights' that students can expect is an open, respectful, tolerant and safe environment in which to learn. Indeed, as witnessed in this case, when students perceive that no such environment exists, they will not 'take chances' or test their partial understandings for fear of being ridiculed. Any group therefore has to balance the need for security (feelings, values) and the need to confront and challenge ideas (see Heron, 1999).

In this case study I had not really thought through the consequences of letting the flame war continue without intervention. While I had prepared and publicized a code of conduct it clearly had minimal influence on what occurred and I needed to resort to official measures to control the situation. If Tony had continued with his attacks, or if others had undertaken further revenge attacks, I would have found myself having to enforce the official position, which may have caused even greater resentment among the students. What started as a minor disagreement between a small group of students could have become a major disciplinary event. One important lesson to learn from this is the speed with which such a situation can develop in an online discussion group.

Passive students who refuse to participate are always a source of frustration for any academic. Many students find the potential embarrassment from publicly expressing their views in front of their peers prevents them from contributing. It is unlikely, however, that any kind of shock treatment will overcome this type of reluctance. While the initial effects of the flame war were to make some students more dynamic, the result for the group as a whole was negative. And it is likely that those students who participated in the flame war would have contributed to debates anyway. On the other hand, those who were already nervous about giving their viewpoints may be even more loathe to participate.

Online learning brings additional factors into disputes between students, including the following:

- In a classroom environment exchanges during an argument are accompanied by visual gestures that help to minimize any misinterpretation of what has been said. Body language can soften the severity of the spoken word. Seeing the other's reaction through their facial expression can indicate that what has been said has unintentionally offended. In an electronic environment, individuals only have the printed word to interpret. It is difficult to include tone or any pacifying gestures in an e-mail message.
- The recipient doesn't have to rely on memory when reviewing what has been said – it's there to be read again and again. Rereading can intensify the reaction in comparison to when the same comment is spoken once. In addition, a printed version takes on a more formal, official identity – it represents a permanent record and this encourages the need to provide a similar response, starting the downward spiral into a heated exchange.
- Internet channels are very public, making it much easier for others to be drawn into an exchange. On campus, an argument between students would only be noticed by those who are there at the time and in the same room. In a mailing list, for example, others can read the exchange later and by adding their views can rekindle the argument even when the original protagonists have decided to stop.
- The machine interface can affect individuals' characters. In the same way that driving a car can make the meek aggressive, communicating through a computer provides a protective barrier between the combatants. Many individuals would never dream of participating in an argument if everyone was physically present, but will allow themselves to attack an individual whose presence is represented only by a name on the screen.
- Many students use nicknames when they are communicating online, which further enhances the feeling of invulnerability and encourages atypical behaviour. Tony and John could be attacking one another in a newsgroup, but still be blissfully unaware of the fact that they sit next to each other in tutorials. People at Tony's office may think of him as a harmless character who would never offend anyone.
- The status of the lecturer can also be diminished in a virtual classroom. The lecturer's electronic presence is reduced to his nickname, which does not necessarily carry the same sense of authority.

The main objective must be to end the public exchange, and officially rebuking individuals can easily 'add fuel to the flames'. Those reprimanded may feel the need to defend themselves in the public forum, while those seeking revenge are likely to publicly state their support for the censure. The corollary in a traditional lecture theatre is rebuking a whole class for the actions or performance of one or a small number of students. In the online classroom, I restricted my communications about each individual's behaviour to just that student, while reminding the entire student body of the need for tolerance and understanding. This ensured that there was little chance of publicly adding more offence to the existing situation. In addition, my private e-mails acted as an example of how disputes can be effectively handled away from the public eye.

Reference

Heron, J (1999) *The Complete Facilitator's Handbook*, Kogan Page, London

CHAPTER 2

DO STUDENTS REALLY WANT TO INTERACT?

Case reporter: Lori Wallace

Issues raised

The main issue raised in this case concerns the provision of opportunities for distance learners to interact with each other, and factors that affect whether or not students take up such opportunities.

Background

This case covers a decade (1989 to 1999) in a distance education unit located in a dual-mode university. The distance education unit offers approximately 170 courses per year. Courses are largely print-based with audio/videotape supports and telephone tutoring. The annual course enrolment in the programme is about 3,000 to 4,500 learners.

PART 1

Each year, the distance education programme received complaints from some students that they missed the interaction with other students that is part of on-campus learning. For example, a student indicated that, while 'distance study allows me the freedom to continue my studies, I so miss the interaction with other students and at times I feel academically isolated'. Another added, 'I'd like to see study groups set up or at least a list of other people in your class. I think this would have been beneficial for me.' Since instructors in the programme and the distance education literature in general support the idea of students being able to interact with each other, the unit responded by putting in place such opportunities.

By 1989, Alf Smithfield had been in charge of the distance education unit for three years. During those years, the unit had undergone considerable expansion (in enrolment, staff, number of courses delivered, and budget). Alf's efforts had been concentrated on setting policy, developing relationships with other faculties and departments, rationalizing the budget, hiring instructional designers and student services personnel, and putting design and publishing protocols in place.

Alf kept up with the distance education literature and knew about the importance of student interaction. The unit continued to receive requests from students and instructors for opportunities for student–student interaction. At a conference, Alf learnt that another institution, similar to the one in which he worked, was successfully using a Student Network whereby students in each distance education class would get a list of the other students' names and telephone numbers. This sounded like a good model and would not require a large budget to set up and maintain. (This was particularly important because Alf's faculty was expected to fully recover its costs through revenue.)

Accordingly, Alf set about developing a Student Network. Alf's staff liked the idea but, since most already had heavy workloads, no one was able to offer to assist with the project. Alf decided to invest some personal effort in order to get the project under way. He hoped that someone on his energetic staff would eventually be able to maintain the network.

Alf consulted with the Dean of Students about the Student Network. Alf indicated that the network would involve taking student names and telephone numbers from a course section list, and distributing these to all students in that class. The Dean balked at this suggestion and refused to let the information be distributed without the distance education programme first obtaining permission from the students to release their names. This seemed unnecessary to Alf since the institution already published a student telephone book, but he knew it would be unwise not to comply with the Dean's request.

Alf was also not prepared for the opposition to the Student Network from a few instructors, who felt that opening up communication between students would result in increased instances of plagiarism. Alf reassured them that the majority of distance education students were adults and were at a geographic distance from one another. Nevertheless, he agreed that all instructors would have the option of not including the Student Network in their courses.

To the distance education staff, these obstacles were resented because they appeared simply to create unnecessary roadblocks to the growth and effectiveness of the distance education programme, and made Alf look powerless. Nevertheless, arrangements were made to deal with these objections. Permission forms were included in the distance education programme guide and in course manuals, and students were asked to return these so that the Student Network list of names and telephone numbers could be prepared.

At that time, students registered by mail and this meant that the Student Network lists could be compiled only after the registration period was complete (two weeks after the start of courses), and then mailed to students wherever they were located, sometimes arriving midway through the term. Moreover, students who returned the permission slip for the network sometimes then received a letter indicating that the instructor in their course was opting out of the network and that no list would be sent to students in his or her course after all.

Even when instructors did agree to participate, however, students often received the Student Network lists past the time when they would have been most useful. Perhaps as a result of this delay, fewer students returned their signed permission forms the following year, making the lists even less useful. The support staff involved with the network also could not make it a work priority because the busy period for it was also the busy period for registration and course manual mailing.

Consequently, staff members began to resent the extra workload of the network and did not feel ownership of it. They were discouraged at the lack of success, but since there was no other option available to put students in touch with one another, the network continued to limp along.

One bright spot on the horizon emerged in that the university was developing a telephone registration system. Alf knew that a network participation (yes/no) question had been incorporated into the telephone registration of another institution, so he enquired whether this could be done at his institution. Unfortunately, by error, the distance education unit had been excluded in the development of the telephone registration system and it was too late for modifications to be made.

Following five years of unsatisfactory performance, the Student Network was quietly discontinued.

Would you have done anything differently than Alf with respect to planning and implementing the Student Network?
If you were going to reintroduce methods to increase student interaction, what strategies would you employ?

PART 2

Three years later, an entirely new approach to student interaction was suggested. A number of Web-based distance education courses had been developed, university policy now encouraged students to use computers, and staff members in distance education with an interest in educational technology agreed to create Web-based student discussion forums as well as a student listserv. There were two types of discussion forum developed: those which were required and graded as part of course work, and those which were voluntary and unstructured, but within the confines of a particular course. In addition, the student listserv provided students with informal access to learners in other distance education courses. While the required course content-focused discussions were considered an important learning tool, it was the unstructured discussions and listserv that were seen to be the vehicles for informal student networking.

The interaction options were widely advertised among all distance education students. The distance education staff felt that finally students could interact easily both inside and outside prescribed distance education 'class' discussions using methods that required fewer hours of staff time to create and maintain.

To what extent do you think the new Internet-based student interaction oppor-tunities will be successful? Why?
Would you have handled these new interaction opportunities differently? If so, what would you have done?

PART 3

After three years of offering the new opportunities for student interaction, the results were still disappointing. The technician monitoring the Web forums and the listserv reported that very few students used any of the voluntary, informal interaction alternatives offered. Alf felt that the same pattern he had observed with the Student Network appeared to be devel-oping with the new approaches.

At this point, it became evident to Alf that there was something wrong with providing opportunities for informal student–student interaction in the distance education unit. He started to question whether students wanted and needed informal opportunities to interact. He realized that research was needed to provide some insight into the puzzling problem of the lack of student participation.

Finding time and funds to gather and analyse data is a problem in any cost-recovery programme. In the distance education unit, staff members are often totally engaged in the everyday administration of the courses and revision and development of course materials. The staff members in this unit were also under the restraints of their collective agreement in that their job descriptions proscribed combining instructional design work (classified as teaching) and research in assigned duties. Employing researchers outside the unit was costly – an important consideration for a cost-recovery faculty.

Eventually, however, some research into learner demographics and moti-vation was undertaken, and the results provided Alf with some intriguing possibilities regarding the reasons why few students use the interaction options that had been made available to them. The study turned up the fact that the mid-1990s demographics of distance learners had changed dramatically. In the 1980s, when much of the distance education policy had been developed, students were over the age of 26, working full time, studying part time and living at a geographic distance from the campus. Students in the 1990s were under the age of 26, living in the city where the university was located, working at least half-time, and were combining on-campus study with distance education courses.

The data suggested that some students in distance education courses might have already developed a network of friends and study mates on campus. For example, a number of respondents in the study reported that they knew others in the course and had planned to take the course with them. Students in professional faculties such as nursing reported that they knew others in the programme and were also part of a professional network. It may therefore be that some distance education students were interacting with one another frequently, but that they did so using methods quite apart from those provided by the programme.

The fact that distance education students were combining heavy study and employment commitments may also be part of the explanation of their lack of informal interaction. These students reported that work commitments and the freedom to choose where and when they learn were the most important reasons for studying at a distance. With competing and heavy commitments for their time, these students may have to sacrifice social networking.

Alf and his staff decided that they also needed to examine the ways in which the informal interaction opportunities for distance learners were developed, presented and maintained. For example, each of the informal interaction vehicles used by the distance education unit was added without a clear, communicated understanding of how each interrelated with other pieces of the learning experience. These interaction opportunities were not part of the instructional design of each course but, rather, were well-intentioned add-ons to serve somewhat vague social/learning objectives.

What investigation could Alf and his colleagues undertake to determine the best way forward?
What is your evaluation of the need for student interactivity and the way it was attempted in this case?
What issues does this case raise for your own teaching?

CASE REPORTER'S DISCUSSION

There are many points on the interaction continuum, with formal, graded, topic-centered class discussions at one end, and informal, voluntary, open one-to-one discussions at the other. The options used by Alf's distance education unit tended toward opposite ends of the interaction continuum, without ensuring adequate provision for modelling and practice with other options. For example, just as interaction in small groups increases the comfort levels and risk-taking of classroom learners, it is reasonable that this step may be necessary for successful Web- and Internet-based interaction.

More survey and focus group research could assist the distance education unit in providing opportunities that are *needed* and which are within its resources. For example, if research supports the idea that students wish to interact in person, and those opportunities are not readily available to them, study and discussion groups could be arranged in various parts of the city or province to facilitate this goal. Alternatively, the unit may discover and need to recognize that many learners take distance courses precisely because they can maximize their time on course goals and minimize social interaction. Also, if Web- and Internet-based interaction options are to become a more useful tool for learners, these must be more fully integrated into the learning experience, even for voluntary, informal options.

At one level, this case is about trying to meet students' needs within a limited budget. At another level, and more importantly, it is about assumptions. Programming decisions should not be based upon assumptions about student demographics and needs (in this case drawn from a few, perhaps unrepresentative students' requests, opinions of staff and instructors, and findings in the distance education literature that may no longer apply to contemporary distance learners). On the other hand, all educational experiences are values based, and part of the learning experience is development of the concept of a community of ideas and practice. The notion of education as a purely 'private' transaction, even if desired by students, can be questioned from a values position. Also, the age-old problem in education of students perceiving that they prefer one thing (perhaps *not* wanting to interact) is often reversed when they actually successfully experience the new thing. Again, however, it can be argued that programming decisions should not be based upon vaguely expressed social objectives, unintegrated 'enhancements' of the learning experience, or unexamined instructional design assumptions: they need deeper and more explicit thought than that.

The underlying instructional design model used in this distance education unit emphasized independent learning for students who are isolated from the on-campus experience. This model was developed to provide access for adult learners who juggled multiple responsibilities including full-time employment, family and part-time study, and who were geographically distant from the campus. While this demographic profile no longer fits the majority of learners in the unit, it is unclear to what extent the instructional design model fits the current population. If the model attracts and reinforces only students who learn independently, is it surprising that many chose not to interact unless required to do so?

Finally, this case points to the limitations of the distance education literature in programme planning. The preponderance of descriptive research limits the value of the literature in guiding the programming of any one unit. Distance education and flexible learning units cannot afford *not* to do institution or unit-specific research. Such research is very necessary to avoid costly programming errors.

As a distance education student would you wish to interact with fellow students? What level of interaction would you demand?

As a distance education teacher, how important would you feel it is for students to interact with each other? What level of interaction would you demand?

What sources of information should a distance education unit use in programme planning and development?

From your experience, does the overall instructional design model used in distance education courses encourage or discourage collaboration among learners?

CHAPTER 3

PACIFIC MAYDAY: CONVIVIALITY OVERBOARD

Case reporter: Roger Boshier

Issues raised

This case study raises issues concerning the use of an electronic discussion group to speak across international borders and how assumptions about expected behaviour can be eroded.

Background

The two graduate adult education groups discussed in this case belong to similar programmes from the University of British Columbia (UBC) in Canada and the University of Auckland in New Zealand. Both overlooked the Pacific Ocean, were immersed in a British Commonwealth tradition and had historical links with each other. Also, there were similarities in literature used in coursework and, in both places, a preoccupation with aboriginal issues.

PART 1

Faculty members in Canada and New Zealand decided to create an electronic *hui*. A *hui* is the New Zealand Maori word for a meeting staged by local people who feed and accommodate what is often a large group. As each group arrives they are welcomed in a ritual that includes calling, wailing, chanting and oratory. These 'rituals of encounter' constitute a balanced exchange between locals (*tangata whenua*) and visitors (*manuhiri*). *Huis* are used for 'big days' – weddings, funerals, meetinghouse openings, political events, birthdays and anniversaries.

The *hui* would foster discussion among our graduate students and we thought there would be little difficulty with the kinds of cultural misunderstandings and enmities that erode conviviality when, for example, Turks talk to Greeks and Israelis talk to Arabs. A short *hui* on a listserv would yield benefits for both sides and show what can be done without flashy Web technologies. Auckland students felt isolated from but interested in other adult education programmes. In Vancouver, there was considerable interest in the South Pacific. The *hui* aimed to foster dialogue. Organizers hoped it might lead to long-term relationships – student exchanges, research projects, collaboration on development projects. New Zealand Maori were already working with British Columbia First Nations (indigenous people). Maybe the *hui* could build on that goodwill.

During a *hui*, various mythological devices are brought into play. While we could not hope to capture the intricacies of a 'real' *hui*, not least of which was feeding all participants, it was the stress on mutual and respectful exchange that seemed to fit what we wanted to do.

Using the Majordomo software, students in both places would subscribe to UBC ADED-NET and discussion could begin. At the Vancouver end, the organizer – a kiwi (New Zealander) who had lived in Canada for 25 years – explained that a *hui* was a respectful, equilibrious exchange. Canadians were happy to sail under the *hui* flag.

In late April 1999, participants were promised, 'This will be all over by May 31. We want a lively discussion but do not want to add to e-mail overload.' Hence, participants were told postings should be one or two pages (screens) long and they were asked to put the subject of their message in the header line. Then, in familiar adult education style, participants in both places would introduce themselves by reflecting on their abilities as a 'lifelong learner'.

Introductions contained a mix of personal and professional information ('I live with my husband and feisty cat... I've worked in three Canadian museums as an educator and curator'; 'I make hand-made quilts with no sewing machine and pester plants in my rocky Gulf Islands garden'). The New Zealand tendency to use *kia ora* (or *kia ora koutou katoa* – 'greetings everyone') as the opening salutation impressed Canadians and showed how Maori-ness had penetrated the soul of *Pakeha* (non-Maori). This emboldened Canadians to post greetings in languages other than English and would later spark a discussion about the Aotearoa (New Zealand) Treaty of Waitangi.

At first, it looked like the *hui* had left the dock in fine style. But hazards to navigation lay ahead. Not rocks or adverse weather. Rather, the crew started to squabble. Two problems showed up immediately – the first involving critique, the second an allegation of 'ranting'.

An Auckland student introduced himself by describing his work with 'a company which provides support for people with psychiatric disabilities'. 'A company? Has mental illness become a commodity?' snorted Canadian Medicare enthusiasts. Was this guy an unwitting accomplice of Milton Friedman and New Right crazies? In Vancouver, a student well versed in discourse analysis jumped on the Aucklander by exposing subtexts he found nested in his psychiatric constructions: 'What kind of life have they had which is so loaded with mental health oppression from societies which tend to exclude, marginalize, and pathologize any "disability" that is outside the norm?... What is your aim in rehabilitation?' Although the Vancouver student said he didn't require immediate answers to these and similar questions, this message landed in Auckland with a boom that rivalled Mount Ruapehu, the local volcano.

A gay man in Vancouver then posted a message about the 'dangerous' and 'oppressive' nature of formal institutions. He was keen on informal and non-formal settings. A heterosexual UBC woman student said that 'rather than rant on about problems in academia' it would be better to focus on the way lifelong education had been hijacked by the consumerist orientation of lifelong learning. In a follow-up message the gay man retorted, 'I can only assume that the "ranting" alluded to, may – in part – refer to my previous message... I think my issues are legitimate; sorry to have them trivialized and minimized (silenced) as rantings.'

On 11 May the author of the 'ranting' message sent a sidebar e-mail to the Vancouver organizer saying her message had been misunderstood. 'This just served to underline the difficulties of using e-mail for education', she said. She was participating reluctantly. And now this!

Rather than rubbing noses, we appeared to be punching them. This didn't look like a *hui* at all. The Canadian who rebuked the New Zealander working with psychiatric patients had apparently not realized 'Round One' involved introductions, not critique. Moreover, he compounded the situation by posting a CV that listed numerous publications. In Auckland, he looked like a hotshot on a mission. 'Wow, what are we into here?' was a common reaction.

The *hui* was barely away from the dock when the gay student considered himself 'trivialized' and 'silenced'. The 'ranting' flare-up might have been routinely defused in a face-to-face environment and dismissed as 'lively discussion'. But 'ranting' now hung like black storm. Was it time to pull the plug?

Why do you think this situation developed?
What options do you see as being available at this point?
What would you do?

PART 2

In Vancouver, the organizer pleaded for civility and encouraged postings from students known to be good at defusing rancour. But, in the middle of all this an Aucklander asked, 'Is it me or do these Canadians sound hard/harsh? Are we Aucklanders being a little mousy and nice?' Later, the Auckland organizer wrote an article that contained a generous interpretation of contretemps in Vancouver, as follows:

> When some of the less experienced (New Zealand) students made their first, tentative contributions introducing themselves and their academic interests, some Canadian participants immediately responded by critiquing their ideas, despite the mediator requesting that everyone confine their first round to personal introductions. Unfortunately, several of the New Zealand participants interpreted these responses as serious challenges about their credibility, resulting in their withdrawing from the rest of the exchange.

Further, during the *hui* introductions the Vancouver organizer received a phone call from a Maori student in Aotearoa. 'We're lukewarm Brits in this part of the world!' she exclaimed. 'Knowledge exists outside ourselves. This personal focus – introducing ourselves – it's embarrassing. Kiwis don't like talking about ourselves. Have you forgotten?' This communication, sufficiently important to warrant a phone call rather than an e-mail, was enough to trigger a Mayday.

Now what? The *hui* was disabled and no salvage company was in sight. There weren't many options. Organizers exchanged sidebar e-mails and resolved to remind participants it would all be over by 31 May. We would try to disperse the cloud by carrying on regardless. Perhaps we were warmed-over Brits and a bit of stiff upper lip might do the trick? So we rehoisted the sails, plotted our position and carried on. Sort of.

Given the unfortunate developments, should the hui *be abandoned?*
What do you think happened next?

PART 3

With some trepidation, the organizers continued with the next question: 'What Does "Diversity" Mean in Your Neck of the Woods?' The question was accompanied by a set-up piece that speculated about homophobia in both places, the burden of credentialism, the difficulties of doing adult education in the context of the New Right obsession with performance, measurement and accountability, and relationships between aboriginality and colonialism.

The gay man on Vancouver Island again weighed in with a 'promise to be good this time around'. His posting violated the 'two-screen' rule but intelligently discussed sexuality in Canada, the role of the federal Charter of Rights and the importance of staying focused on the intersection of location, identity, processes and product in teaching. It concluded with a strong endorsement of non-formal settings for education. Were we back on course?

Then followed a series of exchanges about aboriginal/white relations in both countries and the importance of the Treaty of Waitangi in Aotearoa. Canadian students were sent Pakeha and Maori versions of the treaty. This was a lively exchange. But, just below the surface, participants were still apprehensive about criticism from UBC. Hence, a PhD student prefaced his contribution to the diversity discussion with, 'Well, here's my uninformed and poorly-considered two-bits worth.' An Auckland student, an expert in outdoor education, said, 'Hmmmm, there seems to be a great deal to chew on. Since my self-concept in this environment is already low and I have a reputation (never mind that now) I'll jump in...'. New Zealand participants were walking on *kina* (spiky sea egg) shells and, at UBC – where criticality and deconstruction is the norm – students were tiptoeing in the rainforest.

The Vancouver organizer had posted a message about New Zealand that some felt was infused with romantic yearnings for the past. This prompted messages about the much-vaunted kiwi ability to manufacture miracles out of No. 8 fencing wire. In Auckland, the organizer posted this: 'Methinks you've been away for too long... NZ has changed significantly over the past 10–15 years... We may not be as credentialed as Canada (yet) but I am currently waiting for the first degree in "Problem-Solving with No. 8 fencing wire" with accompanying Qualifications Authority units standards to match.' Moreover, 'the degree of mateship has also decreased with rampant competition being promoted (along with the mantras of "the market knows best", "screw your neighbour before your neighbour screws you")'.

As well as his posting about credentials and mateship, the Auckland organizer reassured the crew. 'I hope that people are not feeling intimidated about contributing to this *hui* (even though I know from my own research that you probably are...). Have a go! Put the dead cat on the table and tell us like it really is!! You have nothing to lose but your reputation and self-concept. Take care out there.'

Take care indeed! Most of the 108 people on the listserv at the beginning of the *hui* were now silent. They'd fled to the friendlier atmosphere of Ponsonby Road (in Auckland) or Kitsilano (in Vancouver). Yet a hard core remained and, despite hesitation in opening sentences and gossip about overly pompous signature files, the diversity discussion produced jaunty exchanges about sexuality, race and, to a lesser extent, gender. The small hard-core group also steered the *hui* quietly through the final topic, dealing with technology.

Given its shaky journey, what should the organizers do to wrap up the discussion?
Had anything worthwhile been achieved?

PART 4

The *hui* had been designed to foster dialogue. Within a short time it had looked dead in the water, a mere shadow of the impressive craft of a month earlier. It had been a struggle marred by incidents but, by 31 May, it had a second wind and was now rounding the breakwater with flags tattered but still flying.

Although few people had participated in the technology discussion and New Zealanders were noticeably absent, some people at both ends felt something had been achieved. Hence, on 31 May the Vancouver organizer requested permission to download hard copies of the entire *hui*. 'In 30 or 40 years from now it might be interesting for folk to see what we in NZ and Canada were talking about at the end of the century.' Several participants applauded the idea of a 'time capsule'. Two Vancouver and two Auckland students had been tasked to 'reflect' on the *hui* process. In both places students took their wrap-up responsibilities seriously. After the usual kinds of statements about how 'interesting' it had been and comments on content, the following points on the process were raised (thanks are due to Eric Damer and Marlene Atleo in Vancouver and Steve Crosby and Nicola Rudge in Auckland):

- The meaning of 'indigenous greetings' (eg *kia ora*) used by New Zealanders was still a puzzle for some Canadians even at the end of the *hui*. But they also suggested Maori in Aotearoa occupied a different position than First Nations in Canada.
- Some introductions looked like a 'brag sheet' and, in New Zealand, participants objected to pompous long-winded signature files.
- Several participants 'talked past' each other ('e-mail has some limitations as a conversation medium,' said one observer). How much were we 'dialoguing' or 'pooling our monologues?' asked a Vancouver PhD student historian.
- Assertive writers cowed some of the less assertive. This was a particular problem for Aucklanders, most of whom were starting a new programme. As one participant noted, 'there is a certain recklessness, spontaneity and anarchy associated with e-mail. These are positive attributes... but some of this seemed to deter participation. Participants who joined the discussion late – and thus missed seeing the ground rules (two-screen limit; stay with the thread; use the subject line) were disruptive and had the potential to derail the process.'

- The Vancouver obsession with criticality and deconstruction can be difficult to manage in face-to-face settings and, in this context, nearly killed the *hui*. In particular, two direct hits nearly sank the ship. Perhaps the notion of *hongi* (New Zealand greeting by touching noses) should have been in the foreground rather than buried under the idea of *hui*? It is hard to hit a person when rubbing noses.

- The organizers did not consider what might happen by mixing up inexperienced (in some cases certificate and diploma) with experienced (eg PhD) students. As an Aucklander said, 'I felt flabbergasted and intimidated by the "language" used in several writings, wanting desperately to respond, yet finding the dialogue difficult to grasp without the ability to ask questions along the way.' Where did the others go? 'One or two felt like me yet could not break in without stating something simple like "What the hell are you talking about?"' Another participant quoted Winnie the Pooh: 'I am a bear of little brain and long words bother me.'

- New Zealanders have a reputation for being direct in social relations. Yet, during the *hui*, it was the supposedly mild-mannered Canadians who aggressively critiqued each other. Why? Perhaps an Auckland student had it right: 'I wonder if the kiwis could be a rather shy, polite and easily intimidated lot, a bit wary of owning their own thoughts? Have the Canadians heard of our "tall poppy" syndrome? ... The Canadians sounded so blunt... and quite threatening at times... what is culturally sensitive/insensitive in Canada cannot be assumed to be the same in New Zealand... and there are cultures within cultures are there not?' This message, posted during the wrap-up on 2 June, effectively tossed another bag of binary oppositions into the discussion.

At the time previously announced, the door of the *hui* slammed shut – with sighs of relief on both sides of the Pacific. Just prior to the closure there was a flurry of e-mails saying, 'it wasn't so bad', 'something had been accomplished', 'we should do it again', 'we learnt something'. Some students kept talking on sidebar discussions and where assistance with assignments was sought, help was freely given on both sides.

What lessons should the organizers take away from the experience?
Does this case provide any insights for your own teaching?

CASE REPORTER'S DISCUSSION

With the insolence of hindsight, it now appears this kind of event would work better if the following were considered:

- Software such as Monash University's InterLearn (see Chapter 13) allows participants to type their contributions into a window. This may constrain the verbose and encourages the timid. It also provides an attractive architecture to encourage reflection and interaction.

- 'Thread-mapping' software (such as UBC's WebCT) would have helped foster a dialogue – rather than a pooling of monologues. Because 'thread-mapping' lays out an architecture for discussion it may have sparked the participation of lurkers who would normally be anxious in unstructured discussions.

- The *hui* was a voluntary activity. Although egos were at risk no marks or course requirements were involved. Hence, there was a certain nonchalance in the interactions which may have been different had assessment or reward been at stake. It was noticeable that the four 'observers' were thoughtful and serious about their responsibilities. Having been tasked to do the wrap-up they had a vested interest in doing a good job.

- It might have been better if someone other than the Vancouver organizer had written the set-up for each question. In too many cases, contributors reacted to his points and did not engage with broader issues lying behind the question. In this case the process might have been better had the convenor been less visible.

- A mechanism to ensure a more equal number of contributions from each place might have militated against the Vancouver flare-up that nearly sank the *hui* in the first week.

- The ground rules (two screens only; use the subject line; stay on the thread; no critique in the warm-up/introductions phase) should have appeared as a recurring tag line. In this way latecomers would be less inclined to throw messy spanners in the works.

If there is one feature that distinguishes adult from other forms of education it is the need to respect learners' experience. Hence, adult educators emphasize interaction. Technology now makes possible discussions that span vast oceans, leap fjords or scale mighty mountains. But, when the usual attributes of discussion are stripped away and all that remains are words on a screen, what starts as cordial conversation can turn into a pub brawl. Speaking across borders has never been easy. Yet there is a continuing need for people of goodwill to keep talking. Conviviality would be a good start.

CHAPTER 4

Do we really need an online discussion group?

Case reporters: Charlotte Gunawardena, Jan Plass and Mark Salisbury

Issues raised

The issue raised in this case is whether active collaboration in group discussions is a necessary component of online courses. Is it necessary for learning, and what particular purpose is collaborative discussion expected to serve?

Background

This case study describes a graduate-level course on Instructional Systems Design (ISD) taught at the University of New Mexico, a large research university in southwestern USA, that enrols a diverse student population. The course, which is also offered as an on-campus face-to-face class, was adapted and designed for the Web environment by Jan, then a faculty member of the Organizational Learning and Instructional Technology Program (OLIT) in the College of Education, and a team of OLIT graduate students. The students who enrolled in this course were motivated, self-directed adult learners who came from the corporate sector, government institutions and higher education. Most of them work full time and have family commitments. All of them had prior experience of participating in the programme's listserv discussions and were familiar with the online environment. For many, it was their first online course. Jan and Mark were experienced in ISD, and in classroom facilitation of this course. While they had been using online materials as supplements for their face-to-face courses, it was the first time they had taught an entire course online. Charlotte provided tips for course design and brought her colleagues together to reflect on the teaching process.

PART 1

It was a great opportunity for online development. We had the course, the experience, the expertise and the resources.

We started with an existing course on ISD from which we designed and developed an online version. The resulting Web-based course is primarily an independent study model, emphasizing self-directed learning skills, drawing on ideas from a number of learning theories, and providing means for active collaboration among peers. The goal of this project-based course is to familiarize students with the theory and practice of the systematic design of instruction. Student performance is evaluated on the final project, in which students develop a complete instructional design document for six to eight hours of instruction.

The online course materials are presented in three sections: the course materials section, the case library section, and the communication section.

The course materials section consists of 16 lessons, each covering a phase of a model of the instructional design process. Each lesson begins with a short introductory video clip, and additional clips feature the instructor connecting theory and practice and making the transition between lessons. A case example is included to help students make the connection between theory and practical application. This section also includes slides, references to the assigned reading, links to other relevant Web sites, and comprehension exercises that provide students with a means for self-evaluation of their learning progress.

The case library section allows learners to view examples of the application of a particular part of the ISD process in various contexts, helping them develop a richer understanding of the particular process or concept, and allowing them to choose case examples that best fit their prior knowledge, experience, or interest.

In order to support networked learning and facilitate interaction between the instructor and students and among students, the communication section includes an online discussion forum with threaded discussions. When we designed the course, we felt that an opportunity to discuss course topics and project issues would support students' learning processes. The discussion forum was designed to provide a collaborative learning environment where students could share any questions they had about the course material and projects, and engage in discussion, helping and supporting each other.

There were no specific goals and objectives for the discussion forum, nor were students required to participate. One reason for the decision not to require participation was the high workload imposed on students for course assignments and the design project. We assumed that students would initiate their own discussions since they were studying at a distance and would have questions to which they could receive feedback from the instructor and from other students. We also thought that the discussion forum would be an excellent space for them to discuss the questions they had about the case studies.

As instructors, we felt the need to design as many avenues as possible for communication between the students and us. Therefore, we designed other means of communication: the possibility for e-mail dialogue with the instructor, face-to-face meetings with the instructor on or off campus, and four synchronous class meetings either face to face for those who could attend, or through desktop videoconferencing for those who could not. In fact, we thought the design of the course had taken care of all the communication needs of distance learners. We provided the discussion forum as a support system for those who would need it and thought it would be put to frequent and good use. Our seemingly well-designed course was ready to run.

What level of success do you predict for the online discussion? Will students initiate online discussion themselves?
What determines whether active learner collaboration in group discussions is necessary for the learning process?

PART 2

At first, it seemed that all was going smoothly. The Web site functioned as designed and the face-to-face sessions were well attended. However, although there were only four face-to-face/desktop video meetings during the semester, these began to assume a higher level of importance than anticipated.

The first course meeting was an orientation and 'get to know one another' session. The other three meetings were each scheduled a week before a major assignment was due. The tone of all of these sessions was one of clarifying expectations for students. The introductory meeting focused on clarifying expectations about the course in general. The other three meetings were concerned with setting expectations for the upcoming assignment. Consequently, the meetings took on a 'question and answer' quality where most of the time was spent detailing what and how much should go into the various aspects of the assignment. Little of the meeting time was used to 'teach content' in the sense of focusing on the reading materials and exercises. As a result, instructors began to feel a certain amount of guilt about not having 'covered' the assigned materials in class – either by lecture or discussion.

The outcome was that the instructors compensated for this by 'over-correcting' assignments. That is, they wrote very detailed comments that directly referenced the textbooks. In addition, one instructor allowed students to hand in assignments for extra credit. Most of this overcorrecting was aimed at teaching the content of the course. In other words, the teaching that was embodied in the review comments on student papers closely resembled the teaching that goes on in the traditional classroom through group participation. Without knowing it, the instructors were trying to 'cover' the assigned materials through an ad hoc method aimed at addressing student misconceptions.

Similarly, the students approached the online course as they had a traditional course. Much like coming to class unprepared, they accessed the online materials before reading the assignments and completing the exercises in the course textbook. This time, however, they found that – unlike a traditional classroom with an instructor – they had difficulty understanding and following the online materials. There was no instructor to 'cover' the materials that they should have read before going online. There was no choice but to go back to their textbook and read the assigned materials and complete the exercises. After returning to the online course, they found that they could easily understand and follow the materials. As a result of this initial experience, they fell into a routine where they completed their offline reading assignments and exercises before going online. Upon hearing this explanation, one of the instructors summed it up as follows: 'Students don't mind wasting an instructor's time in a traditional classroom by coming to class unprepared, but they won't waste their own time by going online unprepared.' Students in this course concentrated their time preparing for the online assignments.

Meanwhile, the online discussion group was languishing. While the instructor valiantly tried to encourage students to participate in the online forum and posted questions to generate worthwhile discussion, very few students posted to the group. The intended collaboration and sharing of ideas and issues simply did not happen as planned.

Naturally this concerned us, and we used the evaluative feedback from the students to try to tease out the reasons for the lack of discussion. One student who completed the course remarked: 'One of the features I found most useful was the teaching slides that were included in each module... Another thing I found helpful was the student projects. We need more student projects online!' Perhaps this student was one of the highly self-directed learners who managed to function well without the discussion group. Another student's evaluative comment on the lack of participation in the online environment provides a further clue: 'I struggled a lot with the case studies. A lot of times there didn't seem to be enough information for me to clearly understand the issues. Sort of like there were pieces missing.' Then why didn't this student go to the discussion forum and post a question about this problem? The same student observes: 'I like the communication features. Unfortunately our class wasted most of the benefit of them complaining about books not being in. There was little discussion of issues of substance.'

Students observed that they would have liked to share and discuss ideas with others, find out how others were doing on their group projects, and feel part of the class community. But was the lack of group participation in this case really a problem? Since students did quite well in the online version of the course, compared to a traditional offering of the course, one might conclude that group participation serves no purpose. However, when analysing student comments regarding the online course, we found that the discussion and teaching of content provided by group participation are just as needed in the online course as a traditional course – although they were achieved in a different way online.

What are the reasons for the lack of student participation in the discussion group?
What advice would you give to the instructors in this case study?
Have you had any similar experiences to those outlined in this case? What did you do?

CASE REPORTERS' DISCUSSION

In a traditional college-level course, we expect that students learn most of the course content through preparation for class meetings by reading materials and completing exercises. In class, the content is clarified and elaborated by lectures and discussions. All instructors know, however, that some students come unprepared for class – they have not completed all their reading and exercises. As instructors, we address this in class by 'covering' the same assigned materials either by design – through presentations and activities – or by ad hoc methods, aimed at addressing student questions. Consequently, instructors and students have come to expect that much of the class time will focus on the discussion of reading materials and exercises.

In the online course, we had designed a threaded discussion capability to provide a means for group participation. This was an attempt to provide a sort of proxy for the group participation that has traditionally taken place in the classroom. What we had perhaps forgotten was that even in the classroom, discussion does not take place spontaneously – it first requires leadership and then facilitation. Hence, as described earlier, the students in the online course did not use the online discussion group. Yet, since they were as successful as students in our traditional course, they must have learnt the course content by different means. That is, the learning of content through group participation that happens in a traditional course was learnt in an individual self-directed learning mode.

It is apparent why active group collaboration as intended in the online discussion forum did not happen. The learners' reliance on their own self-directed learning skills when faced with online assignments, the Web-based materials that supported the course, the overcorrection of assignments by the instructors, and the four class meetings that addressed questions and issues, compensated for the intended online group collaboration.

For highly motivated and self-directed learners who juggle online course work with several other competing duties and demands, the discussion group may not have been enough return for their time investment. In other words, they explored other means of communication before turning to the discussion forum when a need arose. For example, when a student had a question about the needs assessment process, he or she would access examples from the case library before going online and asking the question in the discussion forum. With limited time to spend, students placed lower value on the discussion forum (which wasn't graded) than other methods of communication that were available. These other methods such as e-mail or appointments with the instructor may also have been more personal and relevant to specific issues that individual students had.

There may also have been an emotional or affective aspect to non-use, however, in that entering a new discussion group, as with entering any new social situation, raises issues concerning acceptance, status, fear of appearing foolish and so on. This means that face-to-face 'group building' can be an effective way of ensuring that a discussion group works. We have no way of knowing the effect that such emotional issues had on the development of the group.

In reflecting on student evaluation comments at the end of the course, we realized that although students were able to complete it satisfactorily without the online group collaboration, the facilitation of such collaboration would have increased their satisfaction. And even though some students desired this collaboration, they did not initiate the discussion in the shared group conferencing space.

From early on in the semester, the climate of the discussion group was such that some students thought it would be a waste of time to engage in worthwhile discussion in that space. This points out the importance of 'meaning' that students attach to online spaces, their purpose and usefulness. Once a specific meaning is attached to an online space, it is difficult to change it.

As instructors we did some soul-searching to determine where we went wrong. We realized that we did not give the discussion forum high priority. When our initial attempts to get a discussion going on course topics failed, we let it go, compensating for the lack of participation by other methods we have described earlier. The conference space may have become associated in students' minds as a place to deal with the housekeeping details of running a course such as ordering textbooks, not one that would facilitate higher order cognitive learning. Our reflective discussion indicated that we hadn't given careful thought to three questions as we designed and facilitated the course:

1. What was the objective of the discussion group and how would it contribute to learning in this specific course?
2. Does active collaboration happen naturally, or should it be required as part of the grade?
3. How can we build a sustained online community so worthwhile discussions can take place?

So how would we plan and design the course next time? The most important consideration would be to determine the purpose of online group collaboration. Is it necessary to support the learning processes in the course? We still don't really know this, as we found that some students managed to succeed quite well without the discussion group. We feel that given the content and structure of our course, which was primarily aimed at teaching students how to apply the ISD model to course design, online collaboration may have been just one teaching/learning approach. For example, if the course had been designed to focus on a critical analysis of ISD principles, the online discussion may have been more central to the learning process. Even in our course, however, some students did indicate in their evaluations that they would have liked to have a meaningful dialogue on course topics. Therefore, the necessity for dialogue and collaboration will remain an important component of an online course. Some students need the group affiliation and discussion more than others. We felt that in order to make group collaboration more relevant, not only should we communicate this relevance to the student, but also design the group conferencing space better by assigning different meanings to spaces; a space for housekeeping details, for discussion of course topics, for socializing, etc.

Therefore, the decision to include an online discussion group must be considered carefully, taking into account the characteristics of students, the structure of the content, and the amount of dialogue and collaboration necessary for the learning process. Other questions we need to address are:

- What would the online discussion group achieve compared to other teaching approaches?
- Will other activities compensate for it?
- Will it increase workload for the students?
- How could it support the diverse learners in the course?
- Should it be linked to assessment?

We have also realized that if we decide a discussion forum is necessary, creating a conferencing space is not enough: a community must be built and activities moderated. One of the reasons for non-participation in our case may have been the lack of effort by the instructors to build a sustained online community. In our case, while the teachers encouraged students to introduce themselves and attach their biographies, they did not follow it up by sustained community-building activities throughout the course. Community building would be critically important when there are diverse learners who must feel a sense of comfort in order to participate. We felt we needed to focus on this area the next time around.

Another area that needed improvement in our case was the instructor's role as a moderator. This is a difficult role change when we move from teaching a traditional face-to-face class to an online class. Moderating a computer conference requires great time commitment from the instructor. It would take much more time when compared to moderating a face-to-face discussion. We will need to develop a unique set of skills to communicate and maintain the group process through a text-based medium. The fact that we were pretty good face-to-face discussion moderators did not mean that we would be good online moderators. We felt we needed to develop our online moderating skills and teach our students how to moderate the discussions as well.

CHAPTER 5

Houston, we have a problem!

Case reporters: Catherine McLoughlin and Joe Luca

Issues raised

The issues raised by this case concern the use of an electronic listserv to foster teamwork among adult learners developing project management skills via distance learning.

Background

In an interactive multimedia subject, final year students are required to interact with industry clients and to develop a Web site to fulfil their business needs. The unit of study forms part of a three-year degree in multimedia and communications. Students receive online resources and have access to e-mail for tutor and peer feedback. In this particular unit there were 60 students, most of whom had some work experience, and the age range was about 25 to 35 years. Several multimedia staff members and industry representatives attended the listserv, so students had a large field of expertise available to them when they needed information. There was no formal face-to-face contact with tutors. Although the listserv was used by students mainly to engage in teamwork and share of ideas, learning and management issues were also raised there.

PART 1

When we first started to plan the unit, one of the main questions we asked ourselves was, 'How do we enable or encourage effective online discussions so that our students develop team skills?' We agreed that an electronic discussion would be the best solution for both pragmatic and pedagogical reasons. As this unit aimed to develop students' teamwork and project management skills, we wanted the learning experience to reflect real world communication. The assessment task required students to form teams and to create a Web site for an industry client. By careful unit design and task management we saw teamwork online as readily achievable and conducive to constructivist learning outcomes. For pragmatic reasons, an electronic listserv gave students the scope to brainstorm ideas, to discuss approaches and to collaborate online.

Unlike the other units in the degree programme, this one afforded no face-to-face contact with tutors. However, we thought online communication would provide learners with the opportunity to develop a 'learning community' that would encourage the sharing of perspectives and strategies, and recognize differences of opinion. So how did we plan to proceed? Our first step was to consider how we could provide an experiential learning environment for adult learners who were highly motivated, yet fairly new to online teamwork.

Joe and I had used authentic assessment (real world task as opposed to paper and pencil) in other courses and found that it was practical, realistic and challenging. Our assessment processes were very specific, with marks allocated for effective teamwork and for product development. This integration of process and product was something we had worked on carefully. The process skills that were assessed were the capacity to report on internal team dynamics, communication strategies and conflict resolution. The objective of the online dialogue and teamwork was to facilitate learning and collaboration as follows:

- There would be two-way discussion about conceptual issues of project management and multimedia design between experts and students.
- Each team would be able to showcase their product on a Web site and then offer constructive feedback to other teams online.
- There would be a close link between conceptual and practical issues, achieved through the team-based tasks.
- Student teams would be offered opportunities to build up understanding through discussion with others online.

With this attention to task and assessment design, we anticipated no real problems with the online interaction. As teachers, we had confidence in our capacity to manage the learning event and we intended to monitor the interaction carefully. Nevertheless, we gave the learners enough control and voice so that they would influence the educational experience.

The term commenced, and in the first couple of weeks the teams appeared to function quite well. Each day the listserv was replete with postings describing how teams had allocated roles and responsibilities to individual team members. As moderators, our opening messages conveyed certain values such as tolerance, respect for diverse views, willingness to take risks and commitment to hard work. Nevertheless, some early comments by individuals showed that the listserv was being used to air personal views, problems and perspectives such as this message from Mike:

> I was nominated 'Project Manager' for this unit by my team, but I didn't know the first thing about it! It is a good learning experience though.
> Has anyone got feedback from their tutors saying that you need to put more into your assignments? It's easier said than done! Especially when you're working on 3 units and also working full-time.

As moderators we reflected on whether we were asking students to do too much. Were the content and teamwork too demanding? How should we respond to criticism? As this was a third year unit, we expected that students would have quite an extensive knowledge of project management, and this prior knowledge would be in evidence. However, we also expected that the listserv would have to develop its own sense of direction through the contributions of individual members and their interpretation of the assessment tasks. Joe responded:

> If you are working full time and studying three units you are basically stressing yourself out and probably making your work and study suffer in some way. We assume that you have 8–9 hours to devote to the subject. I know that not all students have the luxury of studying full time, in which case you need to make a judgement about your own abilities and time management skills.

This did nothing but fan the flames of resentment, as Jeremy quickly told us:

> How are we supposed to live? In a cave, hunting and gathering? At the risk of starting a political debate, youth allowance barely pays enough for petrol in the car, let alone the over-inflated cost of food at the cafeteria… I agree that time management is a huge factor in university life, however, you can't blame students for wanting to earn a buck. The world doesn't stop revolving when you're at university…

Another student, Olive, joined in to add some cynicism to the discussion:

> If you have the choice, just concentrate on the study, and stick it out, eat pizza from rubbish bins, wear the same underwear 2 weeks in a row, drink stale beer at fashionable nightclubs…
> Don't let the '2–3 years experience required' put you off, and don't do what your assignments ask for, do MORE!

While we were deciding what to do, another posting confirmed that some students were beginning to tire of the negativity and wanted to get back to the task. Another student, Alison, addressed those students who had complained:

> Take your hard-luck story and tell it to people who actually care, this isn't what this listserv is about and it's already taken away from me time I should have been spending on my project.

At this point we wondered what was going to happen. Would the groups just turn on each other and abandon the idea of teamwork? Our plan to give students a voice was working really well, but would discussion go off the rails?

What do you think are the main issues here?
Could the problem have been avoided? Should it have been avoided?
If you faced this situation, what would you do now?
What do you think actually happened next?

PART 2

Believing in the capacity of our students to be self-directed, we did not intervene when they engaged in social interaction or complained of the stress of combining full-time work with study. We decided to listen to our students in the hope of learning something new. Real conversation, we told ourselves, is not opposition or confrontation, but accommodating. We suspended our beliefs and decided to trust the students in the hope of finding out more about their needs and worries. With Alison's comment and exhortations, a number of students rallied to her side, and asked others to devote time to the task rather than using the listserv for personal expression of viewpoints unrelated to the unit of study. With the imminent arrival of a due date for submission of a project plan for the client, the task seemed to establish a focus for group communication, and there were fewer postings in the category of personal complaints.

As online moderators our role was to facilitate development of a virtual community of learners, and we wanted to avoid being judgmental and critical of students' postings at this early stage. Being positive, we saw this initial round of off-task talk as an indication that the communication channel was working and Alison's message was a reminder to focus on the upcoming task and was taken on board. So we learnt two lessons from this first phase of discussion: first, that a social climate was vital to these students and second, that peers can also be active as moderators of discussion.

We did have some evidence of teamwork when teams posted examples of their project plans for peer comment. Would our role of supporting learning online be limited to sitting on the sidelines observing, merely engaging in management functions? As each team progressively worked with their industry client they drew up a management plan that was posted for comment, and we provided positive feedback. The next stage involved creating the product, usually a Web site, for the client and providing a URL to other students to peruse the site and then post back constructive comments to the listserv. Quite unexpectedly, one team member, Rob, who had been very active and intent on the task, wrote a subject line which read, 'Houston, we have a problem' with the following message:

> What do you say when your team completely falls to pieces and one person tries to take it over? Well this is how our team seems to be working and I for one am not going to be part of it. That's not on! Not only that but one team member gets a kick out of undoing our work and putting up his own ideas. I am having no part of this.

So we had a problem! The 'one person' was Rick, a friend of the client. He had decided that this team's work was not up to standard, and then began making decisions on the product design without consulting the others. Stacey, another team member, joined in to defend Rob:

> I like to be a very neutral person trying to calm the situation down as much as I can, but still diplomatically stressing my view that somebody has done something wrong within the team and towards my associates. But when I receive e-mail that is abusive, tells me that I haven't done anything towards the project, and swearing is included, that is the limit! I allow abuse to a certain point and then react and honestly don't care any more about diplomacy, but I defend myself.

As the third team member, Tim, joined in to attack the culprit (Rick) there seemed to be an overwhelming weight of evidence that teamwork was abandoned and that Rick had decided to take over and change decisions that had been made through the group process. It came as no surprise to us that the other team members had begun to feel resentful and excluded. Worse, the brawl was public and others were beginning to take sides, leading to further backstabbing and personal attacks.

If confronted with this situation, what would you do?
What do you think happened next?

PART 3

The listserv seemed to be heading for disaster, with one team feeling vulnerable about being attacked verbally, fearing that decisions were being made without consultation. The public nature of the dispute had contaminated other groups and resulted in loss of confidence in the communication medium. However, at least one student tried to offer the view that there was still openness and transparency about the communication: 'to the person who thinks that I am speaking behind their back on the listserv, this is an open channel… too bad! It is a good idea to try to work things out'. As all our discussion was open until this point, as moderators we decided to use the medium to resolve the conflict. If Joe and I had chosen to phone the culprit and send out a stiff reprimand, it would have given the message that we too lacked confidence, not only in the medium, but also in our own skills as moderators.

Reflecting on our role as moderators, we realized that at an earlier part of the discussion, our approach was that of task management, occasionally switching to a consultancy role. We diagnosed the problem as follows:

- The role dynamics in this team had degenerated so that there was no longer agreement on roles.
- The boundaries between roles had become blurred so that one person was usurping the roles of others and imposing his ideas.
- Relationships began to deteriorate as team members no longer seemed to complement each other. Competition had replaced cooperation.
- Conflict emerged as team members experienced lack of trust and uncertainty, with the additional stress of not knowing whether their contribution would be valued.

So what did we decide to do? My first thoughts were: 'We need to restore a feeling of psychological safety to these students. Ok, the listserv has been abused by one or two to attack others, but equally it can be used to restore harmony and a sense of shared purpose.' Easier said than done, was Joe's answer. But we sat down and revisited our rationale for the listserv, and how we decided to use a set of learner-centred principles to design the learning tasks, assessment and the whole experience. If the students were to remain at the centre of the learning experience, we needed to assert that this was the case, and give them the scope to resolve this conflict themselves. In addition, not all the teams were dysfunctional! Many teams were effectively self-managing their own learning and communication needs. Looking on the bright side, we began to see that the conflict had brought about several unique and unexpected learning opportunities.

'So', I said to Joe, 'Relax! Lets not worry about perfection. Our students are now faced with a real issue of conflict resolution. Which way are we moving? Can we use this situation to enhance learning and sharpen the realization of teams that collaboration is not all that easy?' We could not hide the fact that conflict had occurred, so we decided to use it to our advantage. We advised all groups that successful completion of the assessment task was mandatory, and that if conflicts arose, they had to be resolved internally. Many teams were still working away on their Web sites, and team-based learning was clearly successful for some. The team where the problems had occurred (Rick's team) was given a turn to present the product they had been working on. This allowed them to display their plan, Web site and rationale. Other students received the product with mixed reviews, which allowed the other members of the problem team to demonstrate their skills in design and to return to the drawing board.

We then asked the online groups to consider how best to work in teams and encouraged group discussion of conflict resolution. We invited all teams to share their experiences of how they resolved conflicts and issues, with the aim of bringing out into the open pathways for improved communication and cooperation. This brought about another wave of postings to the listserv, such as the following:

> In my personal experience, I believe the skills needed to work effectively as a team are developed over time and we have been lucky enough to have this year to shape up and prepare for the real world... (James)

> Instead of naming names, blaming, and producing an all out brawl, the team should sit down and be led by one person initially, brainstorm and analyse the various phases of the completed project and then suggestions are made as to what contributed to the team's success or what caused the disaster, if there was one. (Trevor)

> In our project it wasn't one individual but the whole that realized the depth of the problem and devised the solution for our site. A long-winded way of saying this is that our product was a collaborative team effort where ideas are elaborated, refined, abandoned, perfected, abandoned, etc until a final solution was reached. (Marg)

This exercise had a cathartic effect and more positive feelings began to emerge about the process. In fact, the reflective process of seeking openness on the problem team's progress, warts and all, was something all groups seemed to enjoy. So the listserv was back in action and serving the learning needs of both teams and individuals. We had survived the hiccups and interpersonal dramas.

What lessons might e-moderators learn from this experience?
What does it tell you about the problems of teamwork online?
Can students be left to themselves in an online discussion, or does there need to be teacher direction?

CASE REPORTERS' DISCUSSION

From the point of view of designing and planning the learning environment, our initial focus on tasks proved a good starting point. In the first round of discussion, where students began to quibble about the hardships of study and excessive assessment demands, we did not try to stifle these contributions. Our initial commitment to student-centred learning was continued systematically throughout the whole unit, as we believed that a learner-centred environment offered the most appropriate pedagogy for adult experiential learning. (See Bonk and King, 1998, for discussion of how the cognitive, metacognitive, motivational and affective concerns of learners can be integrated into a learning setting.)

Our hunch was that if we gave students control over the listserv, that is, if we gave them boundaries to work within and a task focus, they would use it effectively. We had confidence that students would return to the main agenda of the unit, which was to work in teams to create a product for a client. Ultimately it was students who asserted that others should stop the negativity and return to the task ('This is not what the listserv is about...'). As moderators, allowing students to steer the group back towards the task worked well and affirmed their status as adult learners.

The initial conversations showed that the teams had a number of transition points. Initially, there was a feeling that the unit was all too much, and that tutor expectations were far too great, leading to individual postings. Airing of views probably created feelings of group solidarity, though the chat was 'off-task'. As moderators we trusted the groups to form through this initial phase of socialization.

We looked at the interplay of emotions and learning. For the most part, we noticed curiosity, fascination, engagement, confusion, enthusiasm, anxiety, boredom, frustration, disappointment, insight, satisfaction, and both positive and negative demonstrations of confidence in the listserv. So what did we do? First we emphasized the importance of roles within teams and the importance of being clear about how roles and responsibilities are delegated and carried out. The assessment tasks were designed to affirm role maintenance, while allowing students to build cohesion within teams around individual strengths and interests.

When the team problem occurred and individuals wrote abusive comments, anxiety and disappointment were evident when participants felt their efforts were not appreciated. We realized that negativity can easily creep in, poison relationships and arrest learning. Again, we turned to task and role maintenance, and tried to refocus the groups without appearing too heavy-handed. By fostering reflective, open comments on group processes we conveyed the message, 'Hey, it's OK not be a perfect team... but don't make enemies.'

As group and individual postings showed, there was a mix of feelings about the benefits of group work, but the majority realized that this experience was 'a real world experience' and that teamwork is the responsibility of everybody, not a magic formula that changes individuals into partners overnight.

We allowed as much interaction as students wanted, and rarely intervened to inhibit or limit contributions. Was this a good approach? We believe it was, as we wanted the whole process to be team centred and collaborative. Initially, we were a little too concerned with keeping the discussion away from the personal and the interpersonal. In fact these interpersonal dynamics brought teams together and consolidated online relationships. We experienced gut-wrenching moments when we could feel the discussion going off on a tangent. Our first reaction was to intervene and say to the groups, 'Enough of this!' However, if we had done so, it would have betrayed a lack of trust in our learners, and a departure from our belief that e-learning is a unique context where learner-centred principles mean that students become the centre of the learning environment. Although we chose to be non-interventionist, there was another choice we could have made. We could have intervened in a non-directive way by saying, 'Now what we are seeing here is a breakdown of team skills and communication. How can we resolve this?' It might have worked, but we decided to focus on the task and at the same time give groups the opportunity to use their expertise and experience to reflect on and share the experience of how their own team functioned.

One question we still ask ourselves is, 'How do we create a psychologically safe environment online, and yet not protect participants from the natural cut and thrust of human interaction when groups try to form and create a joint product?' In the course of the semester, one team fell apart briefly, but with mediation it survived. We believe that flexibility, a clear task focus and attention to roles and responsibilities where students act in partnership with others towards a common outcome creates a positive e-learning environment.

Next time round, what would we do differently? Certainly, going into the unit as moderators, we didn't have clear ideas as to what our roles might be. We saw ourselves mostly as electronic mentors, able to give advice when needed, but hoping to be non-interventionist. In our experience, this team-centred environment online showed us that the moderator needs to balance three overlapping process roles: task orientation, social organization and management of learning needs. Easier said than done!

Reference

Bonk, C J and King, K S (1998) *Electronic Collaborators: Learner centred technologies for literacy, apprenticeship and discourse*, Lawrence Erlbaum, Mawah, NJ

TEACHING AND ASSESSMENT ISSUES

CHAPTER 6

TEACHING ONLINE... RELUCTANTLY

Case reporter: Bob Fox

Issues raised

This case raises issues concerning the appropriate use of online discussion groups. The issues include the challenges facing academic staff who are directed to use a particular approach to teaching without adequate preparation, the reconceptualization of teaching provoked by using the technology, and the effects on students and other staff members.

Background

John is a lecturer in the School of Business at an Australian university where he teaches a third year unit in contract law. In his late 40s, John has been a teacher for 20 years, during which he has experimented with a variety of techniques to interest his students in the subject area. The case outlines how John, when directed by his institution, reluctantly introduces online technology into his class of around 40 students. The class gender balance is predominantly male with about one third female in any given year and the ages range from students in their early 20s to their mid-30s.

PART 1

John firmly believed that it is important to engage students in debate and to make learning a student-centred experience. One of the most successful strategies that he had employed for stimulating student discussion was the use of contract law case studies as a basis for student investigation and interaction. In John's experience, students became highly involved in the subject area and participated well in open, live debate.

The university had been encouraging staff to develop more flexible learning courses, providing students with a greater choice of what, when, how and where they study. The use of communication and information technologies in teaching and learning had also been strongly promoted. As part of the strategic plan the university had stated that it expected its graduates to be computer literate and familiar with communication and information technologies; that students should be able competently to communicate, collaborate and cooperate online in the way in which they could expect to work in the 'real' world, post tertiary study.

John was reticent about using online technologies in his teaching. His school, however, had developed an affirmative action plan towards online teaching and his head of school had required all unit coordinators to place their study materials on the Web, linked to the school's home page. The school provided a standardized 'shell', which included online discussion groups in order to facilitate interaction between staff and students. John was strongly opposed to such action, viewing the directive as a waste of time, both for himself and his students, and a waste of money and resources.

John thought that the pressure to have a Web presence derived more from a marketing initiative to attract potential students than from a real desire to improve student learning. He saw his resistance to the use of online technology as educationally responsible and took the view that his head of school was making an impulsive lunge for the latest 'must-have' educational technology. 'Technology for technology's sake', he said. Nevertheless, he bowed to pressure and had a Web site created for his unit, and his colleagues similarly obliged by making the contents of their courses available to students online.

John's colleagues concentrated on placing content in the form of lecture notes and PowerPoint presentations. John, however, minimized his online content, concentrating on short paragraph descriptors of, and links to, key external resource sites in the subject area together with an online discussion forum for students so that they might interact with each other.

It was during a face-to-face tutorial the following semester that students raised a question concerning an online case study that one of them had found on the Web and had referenced in the online discussions page of the unit. Several of the students had started a debate within the online discussion group, based around what they described as 'red button' issues. John was not aware of the case study, nor the student conversations online, so after the tutorial, he went to see what the students had been doing.

He read the case study and the students' online interactions. He was surprised by the quality and depth of the debate between them and felt compelled to react to one or two of the comments. To his continued surprise, several days later he found that students had responded to this and had invited him to correspond again. John found he was being drawn into the online conversation with his students and that the issues raised in the online debate warranted further discussion in the face-to-face tutorials. This in turn encouraged more students to interact in the online debate. What started as a student-led initiative continued for the remainder of the semester, and John's views of the potential of online environments and particularly the conferencing facility, began to change.

However, when he encouraged his students to initiate an online debate in the following semester, the result this time was different: no student took up the challenge and no messages were posted online.

In your experience are 'conversions' such as John's common?
Why do you think John's first online discussion experience was so positive, and his second experience so negative?
What do you think John will do?
What would you do?

PART 2

Faced with the situation of students not taking up the discussion group opportunity, John asked himself a number of questions, such as:

- 'How can I stimulate quality interactions online between students?'
- 'How can I encourage lurkers (students who have not actively engaged in the discussions, but who read the interactions of others) to become active participants?'
- 'Should I consider formally assessing students' interactions in the online discussions?'

John reflected on the paucity of online student interactions in the second semester. Having seen the lively online debate in the first semester, John had identified a potential benefit to his students' work and wanted to continue exploring the possibilities. One point he had recognized was that online discussions were not the same as debates created in face to face seminar environments. The online discussions were a hybrid, somewhere between talking face to face and writing. Online technology provided a different opportunity – not one that replaced existing environments such as the seminar, but one that created a potentially exciting stimulus for students prior to or in conjunction with face to face debate. John also felt that the online discussion group preferred a certain way of communicating and this provided a valuable addition to discussions in the classroom. He summed up his thoughts as follows:

> I don't see this environment as 'virtual' as so many people have said. Students engage in issues as fiercely as they would in the live seminars, but it's different. When you can't see the people you are interacting with, when you can't hear

their intonation, their stress patterns in the language, it's different, but it's not virtual… it feels very real. Students still can get very upset with each other's comments. It's also easy to misinterpret what is said. This way of communicating has its own rules, its own grammar, which does not necessarily mirror face-to-face or conventional communications, like talking on the phone. But what happens in these online discussions has benefited the face-to-face seminar debates no end. I therefore want to continue to use this new environment to stimulate discussion, but I'm just not sure how.

John asked some of his colleagues about ways in which they had used online discussion to get students actively involved. He found that no one in his school could add anything he felt was worthwhile. On the other hand he attended a seminar conducted by a science teacher who had used online discussion groups extensively with postgraduate students and the ideas offered here he found very thought provoking. This seminar led John to consider a different approach to using the technology in the next semester. In particular, he took from the seminar three key points to consider for the following semester.

First, as he had discovered, students are not necessarily going to start to interact with each other online unless there is an 'additional value' for doing so. John concluded that he needed to make the additional value clear. He drew up guidelines and a rationale for interacting online and provided students with some directions and a stimulus to start discussing issues. 'It's obvious to me now,' says John. 'Just expecting students to start debating online is like putting students into an empty room, closing the door and telling them to get on with it! They need some direction and this is what I intend to give them.'

Second, John collected and built in a set of 'red button' issues for students to discuss online, including those covered by the first semester students, thereby providing a stimulus for interactions that would hopefully flow back into the face-to-face seminars.

Third, and again following the advice of the science teacher to outline broad criteria for assessing student interactions online, John made engaging in the online discussions a compulsory and marked form of assessment, constituting 15 per cent of the unit's final marks.

How do you feel about making engagement in the online discussion part of assessment?
What do you think happened when the unit was offered the following semester?

PART 3

After some preliminary confusion among students and a need to clarify the guidelines, John was pleased with the students' initial response to his new approach. By the end of week four all students (43) had interacted in various degrees online. But a new problem arose. The discussions were dominated by a few students, who wrote long and complex messages that took a long time to read through and were difficult to respond to. Also, the conversation thread was frequently lost or hijacked by a few students on a pet topic. John found it necessary to interact online to try to resolve the communications 'spaghetti junction' and to provide some 'model' responses. He also felt he should address some of the more heated debates on sensitive issues. Some students were making inappropriate comments, and verging on becoming too personal.

Reading student messages, following the discussions, interacting and composing model replies were all taking an increasing amount of John's time. In fact the only way he could adequately deal with the work was to spend extra hours at night and over weekends, clearing, sorting and responding to students' comments. His work time had begun to encroach in a big way on his personal time, particularly in the evenings when he found himself glued to the computer screen, searching for answers and producing guidelines for his students. Halfway through the semester, John realized that he had not found a solution but had created a new problem, and a monster at that. Overall, he felt the student interactions were worthwhile, though some students dominated the discussions. However, he needed to find a way to use the technology to engage and benefit his students without creating a huge burden for himself, and he needed a prompt solution.

John contacted the science teacher again to see whether he had come across a similar problem and if so, how he had overcome it.

How would you deal with the domination of a few students and encourage the less forthcoming ones to participate more?
How could John continue to monitor and influence online interactions and yet avoid the huge burden on his time?

PART 4

In the guidelines John included a framework to which students should adhere when composing their responses. This included a word limit within each interaction as well as a limit on the number of responses to each of the red button issues.

Students who wanted to engage in interactions online on other topics were given an opportunity to do so via a separate discussion group. John's unit now had a social and/or general discussion forum as well as the red button discussion forum.

John shared his experiences with colleagues in his school. They were less than impressed. 'You've created a rod for your own back,' was one comment.

'Your experiment with student-centred learning has backfired,' was another. 'Your unit is more teacher-centred than it was before!'

In order to reduce lecturer interactions, John asked students to form groups and to appoint a coordinator for each discussion topic. The coordinator's role was to summarize the discussions at set periods through the semester. In this way, John felt he needed to interact far less than he had previously done. He felt that this provided more student control over their online discussions and in part addressed the criticism of the unit becoming more teacher centred.

John found that marking the online assessment continued to prove problematic, though students on the whole seemed happy with the outcomes. His marking was based on student ability and willingness to communicate, collaborate and cooperate 'appropriately', the quality and depth of interactions online and a demonstration of an understanding of the issues discussed. As the marks only constituted 15 per cent of the total, students were marked leniently. John made a note to talk further with the science teacher who had devoted 60 per cent of a postgraduate unit's marks to student interactions online.

John is still not convinced he has got it right, nor has he mastered the use of the technology. He feels that working in an electronic environment requires ongoing tinkering, an open mind and continuous change. 'So much for the managers' hopes that this technology would reduce our (teacher) involvement,' sighs John resignedly. 'It's always going to take up heaps of my time... much more, in fact, than if I'd never started using the technology in the first place!' However he still believes that 'the benefits of using online discussion outweigh the disadvantages'.

In discussions with his colleagues, John stresses how differently he has applied the technology for teaching and learning purposes. His colleagues predominantly used their unit Web sites 'to place lecture notes and PowerPoint slides of lecture presentations to accompany their unit outlines, online,' says John. Some colleagues had extended their use, by developing multiple-choice questions (MCQs) that the Web courseware tool easily allowed them to develop. 'But essentially, they are teaching the same way that they always did,' says John. 'What they've done is bolt on the technology in an additive fashion... not that there's anything wrong with that, though it seems a waste of an opportunity.' In querying why his colleagues had developed MCQs, John states, 'it's more to do with the ease of making MCQs than any teaching or learning value in MCQs *per se*'. The courseware tool 'allows you to make MCQs easily and so it seems, that's why they are so popular,' he concludes. John questioned his colleagues about the value of the MCQs and he feels no one has been able to provide him with a worthwhile answer. He senses that they are used 'because they are easy to make... and I suppose it provides their students with some level of interaction'.

More recently, John's colleagues have spoken less cynically to him about his use of online discussion and, in particular, the high level of meaningful interactions between students. One colleague confided that his students have started placing pressure on other lecturers in the school to incorporate John's approach to using the Web and in particular the inclusion of online discussions. 'I'm now heralded as an innovator,' laughs John. 'I have to admit, my teaching style has changed because of my involvement with online discussion'.

Will the implied change of heart from John's colleagues continue?
Are there further adaptations that John might make to his approach to online teaching to enable him to lessen the 'heaps of time' that are currently required?

CASE REPORTER'S DISCUSSION

Tenner (1996) in his book on the revenge effects of technology, states that the more sophisticated the technology we use, the more complex the questions we need to ask and have answers for. John's experiences would certainly match Tenner's rule of thumb. But does trying out new technologies always have to be complex and difficult to control? Certainly John found this to be so. However, we all know of lecturers who have many more students than John and who appear to use the technology efficiently (for example, University of Illinois, 1999). In John's case electronic technology provided a new opportunity and a stimulant for students to engage in discussions on the topics he had provided. He realized that the new technology does more than add to the existing teaching and learning environment. It changes the environment in ways we cannot possibly predict:

> I'm tempted to compare the introduction of electronic technology into my unit with the introduction of rabbits to Australia, or European diseases to the Indians in North America. The effects were unforeseen and irreversible... Fortunately the consequences of introducing online technology into my classroom, though unforeseen and numerous were much more positive. The quality and depth of discussions online between students is greater than anything I have encountered in straight face-to-face classroom environments. The ability to think first before composing a question or a response to someone's comment adds the deeper, more reflective and considered dimension that is so important in my subject.

Berge and Collins (1995), among other teachers and researchers, support John's view of the potential added depth of discussion in online environments when compared to face-to-face seminars.

The complexity of the technology and the question of how to use it effectively raise others issues too. We learn to teach by the way we were taught, by our experiences as students, by interacting with our colleagues, by the experiences and work of others that may (or may not) have been analysed and written up. In this new environment, it seems the rules have changed. We can no longer rely on our own experiences. Few university teachers have ever been students in online courses. Few have much experience in this new environment, yet an increasing number of teachers and their students rely on the new communication and information technologies in teaching and learning. John's experiences taught him how important it was to devote more time to preparation, to reduce wasted time during the semester, to unravelling problems and answering additional questions. New conventions, new rules and a new grammar needed to be developed, articulated and learnt. In fact a new way of working and a new way of thinking about teaching and learning are needed if we are to take full advantage of new possibilities.

It was also true that John was fortunate in being offered competent and ongoing technical support to help him update, change and maintain his teaching Web site. Schools of Business in most universities tend to be considerably richer than other schools. Not all university schools are capable of providing this kind of technical and financial support on an ongoing basis. Few teachers are likely to be given such support.

Finally, as with many others, John became caught up in the complex issue of making the discussion part of assessment. Whether this was successful from both the teacher and students' point of view is a key concern that produces a variety of responses. He also faced and at least partially overcame the problem of the dominance of some students, and the need to encourage others to join and post.

References

Berge, Z and Collins, M (eds) (1995) *Computer Mediated Communication and the Online Classroom*, Hampton Press, Cresskill, NJ

Tenner, E (1996) *Why Things Bite Back: Technology and the revenge of unintended consequences*, Knopf, New York

University of Illinois (1999) Report of the University of Illinois teaching at a distance Internet seminar, December (http://www.vpaa.uillinois.edu/tid/report/toc.html)

CHAPTER 7

TRY, TRY AGAIN!

Case reporters: Stephanie Tarbin and Chris Trevitt

Issues raised

The issues raised in this case are student resistance towards the introduction of an online discussion group and the need for balance between academic development objectives and catering to student concerns.

Background

Medieval history is taught as a year-long first year university course enrolling 60 to 90 students. The students comprise a mix of a majority of school leavers and others, many of whom study part time while undertaking paid work. It is taught by John, a senior academic and Stephanie, a junior academic, who was the primary instigator for introducing e-mail discussion groups into the course. Stephanie enjoyed strong support from her colleague and encouragement and practical assistance from her co-author, Chris, a member of the Academic Development Unit. While both Stephanie and Chris have contributed to all of the text that follows, Parts 1 to 3 are told from Stephanie's perspective, and the Case Reporters' Discussion is told from Chris's point of view.

PART 1

Tutorials can be the most exciting and rewarding elements in teaching a course: they can also be the most frustrating. At the end of my first semester of full-time teaching I felt I had experienced both the rewards and the frustrations. I believed that there was room for improvement in the quality of tutorial discussion and suspected that at least some of the students thought so too. Normally a 10 to 15-minute presentation was made by a student at the start of each class, but the 50-minute classes did not seem long enough to explore issues in depth. It was difficult to involve all the students in the discussion as the tendency was for presenters to 'carry' the discussion during the week of their presentation and then to sink back into silence in subsequent weeks.

Reflecting on the semester with John, we agreed that it would be good to create opportunities for students to discuss course-related issues outside tutorial time. We thought that if students who were preparing presentations were able to discuss them *before* a tutorial, then they might identify ways to involve more students in discussion during class.

The idea of an e-mail discussion list was, and still is, attractive to us. We hoped that students would:

- continue debating issues outside the tutorial, and perhaps generate new topics of inquiry;
- cooperate to solve problems together, without necessarily having to collaborate on group presentations or assignments;
- take more time to think through their ideas and to refine their understanding through debate with other students;
- use written debate and archived discussions to develop an understanding of the process of historical interpretation; and
- be inducted to a form of communication increasingly used in most workplaces as well as by historians.

Since I initiated the proposal and was familiar with academic e-mail discussion lists we agreed that the trial would be limited to the 45 students with whom I had contact in tutorials. The practical aspects of managing an e-mail list proved quite straightforward, but we scheduled the e-mail list 'experiment' for the second semester, reasoning that this would enable us to consult the students about their reactions to the idea, to arrange some technical support if needed and also give the students time to settle into university life. We also wanted to elicit students' views as to whether they thought that participation should be part of the assessment structure, and if so then what form this should take. There was a range of responses to our initial questions:

- some students described themselves as technophobic and were worried that their lack of computer competence would detract from their abilities in history;
- others were cautiously interested in what was perceived as a novel and 'modern' approach to medieval history;
- a small group were very enthusiastic; and
- two students resolutely declared that they had no desire to participate.

There was broad consensus that the e-mail list should be a voluntary and unassessed element of the unit. For those wanting an introduction to e-mail, two hands-on workshops were organized in the early weeks of the semester, scheduled outside of contact hours. Some students were strongly opposed to discussing issues relating to tutorial presentations prior to the tutorial class, preferring to establish 'ownership' of particular ideas before sharing them in public. Consequently, we suggested that the students might use the list to debate issues relating to tutorials and presentations. We hoped that our response to the concerns voiced by the students would help to secure commitment to the trial, even though the e-mail list would be less integrated into the unit than we had originally envisaged.

In the event, less than half of the students involved in the trial subscribed to the list and only a handful posted comments on tutorial topics or other course-related issues. The rate of posting was sporadic at best and there was little in the way of debate or exchange of ideas.

At the end of the semester the students told us of the numerous obstacles to their participation. Computer access and technical support on campus were major concerns, often because they appeared unaware of the university facilities available to them. While some students elected to access their e-mail off-campus, most relied on using campus facilities. Other obstacles related to students' approaches to study or to personal habits of organization. Some commented that it had not occurred to them to solicit feedback on presentations or essays; others noted a preference for working independently, or for discussing problems with friends rather than a 'faceless' network of list-members. A number of students also professed intentions of joining the e-mail discussion, and ascribed failure to participate to 'laziness', inability to change existing routines, or lack of organization and time management. Another reason expressed for not taking part in the e-mail discussion was its lack of vitality or 'critical mass'. One student said, 'I suppose if I had heard people raving I might have thought about it but there didn't seem to be much enthusiasm or excitement surrounding it.'

The unmistakable message was that the discussion did not 'take off' because there was no clear or compelling reason to be involved. The e-mail list was extra to the unit, rather than being an integral part of it. For some it was extra 'value', in that it provided opportunities for more discussion, access to peer support and exposure to a greater range of ideas; but for many it was simply more work which was not clearly related to the study of medieval history. Strongly voiced concerns about the ownership of ideas and about the issues of assessment and compulsion persisted, with more speaking in favour of assessment as an 'incentive' for participation compared to before the trial. The outcome of the innovation thus fell well short of our initial plans and expectations.

Given this experience would you continue with the e-mail list or abandon the idea?
If you continued what changes would you make?

PART 2

Despite the discouraging initial attempt, we decided to continue trying with the discussion group in the following year, while responding to the concerns raised by the previous year's students. This meant that:

- the e-mail list had to be part of the assessment structure without being compulsory;
- it had to provide for people who wanted to establish their ownership of ideas;
- the provision of appropriate technical support for students had to be reconsidered; and
- there needed to be a structure for the discussion so that the e-mail list clearly formed a coherent part of the unit as a whole.

To incorporate the e-mail list into the unit as an integral element we designed a semester-long, written debate for the second half of the year on the theme, 'What were the Middle Ages?' This question was the basis of a one-hour test at the end of the second semester and the debate was intended to help students develop their responses. The emphasis of the debate, we wrote in the unit course guide, was on 'the process of clarifying ideas, developing arguments and evaluating interpretations'. The e-mail list was recommended to the students as the obvious forum for the debate and the exercise was awarded a participation mark (10 per cent of the year's work). Students who wished to establish the originality of their ideas were invited to submit their contributions directly to their tutor before e-mailing to the list. If students did not want to engage with the technology, they could submit their contributions as hard copy.

Students were required to complete a two-part exercise involving an e-mail/written component and a tutorial component. First, they were asked to choose a tutorial topic and to write up their 'hypotheses' about its significance. These contributions were to be submitted at the start of the week of the relevant tutorial. Contributions submitted as hard copy were stored in a resource room for medieval history students where they would be available for consultation.

Second, in the ensuing tutorial, students were to identify a significant piece of evidence in order to initiate discussion of specific issues that had helped to form their written hypotheses. For example, a student tackling the tutorial topic, 'The Manor: Rural Society in England', prepared by reading the recommended texts and considering questions about the social and legal status of villeins (the highest or wealthiest class of peasant) compared to freemen, the role of women in rural society and peasant standards of living. At the start of the week they would e-mail their thoughts about the importance of rural society in the Middle Ages. Then, in tutorials, they would identify a piece of evidence for consideration by the class and explain its significance. We asked students to complete this two-part exercise for two of the 13 tutorial topics scheduled for the semester. Additionally, the students who opted for e-mail were asked to make a third post outlining some of their conclusions about the Middle Ages toward the end of semester, but were not penalized if they did not.

Finally, we tried to give the students a range of incentives for using the e-mail list in preference to submitting hard copy. We:

- stressed the opportunity it afforded students as a means of preparing for the final test;
- encouraged informal 80–100-word e-mail contributions but asked for about 400 words if they opted for print;
- presented the e-mail debate as a constructive challenge and an 'experiment' in which we were all (students and staff) engaged together;
- emphasized that e-mail was an increasingly ubiquitous element in modern working environments;
- made systematic efforts to address student concerns about accessing computer labs and technical support;
- supplied them with written instructions for using e-mail and the discussion list; and,
- made two computer-class bookings each week to ensure a minimum level of access to campus machines.

We reasoned that all these measures should help achieve a 'critical mass' in the e-mail debate.

The structured e-mail debate in the second semester was a success in terms of participation. Of the 44 students who completed the course, 37 chose to submit their contributions by e-mail. Over the semester the students posted 153 e-mails, an average of four e-mails per student. The much greater participation in the e-mail debate in semester two thus confirmed our earlier experience that students needed a structured context before posting to an e-mail list.

The final test papers generally developed thoughtful and well-integrated arguments that were supported by a wide range of examples studied throughout the course. Insofar as it was possible to attribute this to the e-mail discussion we thought that the ongoing debate had enabled students to make connections between different tutorial topics and themes. This perception was shared by the majority of students surveyed in the final week of the semester. In a questionnaire distributed before the test, two-thirds of respondents agreed that debating 'What were the Middle Ages?' had helped to link themes and issues in the course. A similar response was given to the statement, 'Composing e-mails helped develop my thinking and clarify my arguments in history', suggesting that the students attributed some value to the expression of their thoughts in writing. As a number of students had e-mailed their tentative hypotheses about the significance of the Middle Ages to the discussion list, we also believed that the exercise had helped some students to refine their interpretation of the period.

Reflecting on this second iteration, we felt that we had attained our teaching aims while respecting student concerns. Technical problems and access to computers continued to be nominated as 'frustrations', although students also expressed appreciation of our efforts to provide support. An experienced student commented: 'Good to learn to use e-mail in first year. Was pretty intimidating at first… this way you get help with it and are not just thrown in to work it out yourself.'

There was little comment on the issues of assessment or compulsion, suggesting that the option of submitting contributions in traditional rather than electronic form provided an acceptable compromise for students who were strongly opposed to using e-mail. Interestingly, the issue of intellectual ownership did not arise at all in comments from this student cohort. Instead, students commented positively on the range of interpretations that the e-mail discussion group presented and the ability to discuss issues without the time constraints of tutorials.

There were two areas in which we felt that we had not achieved our initial goals. First, while we had secured student participation, we felt that the quality of interaction between students had not been that high. For example, most students e-mailed their thoughts on a topic to the list without relating them to the ideas expressed by others, so that the 'debate' became little more than a series of utterances lacking explicit connection. Some of the students commented that there needed to be more engagement with other's arguments; one suggested that if two posts were made per person per topic, the second contribution could involve 'critical analysis of someone else's first post'.

Second, the two-part exercise was too complicated, or too difficult, for the complementary relationship between tutorial and e-mail discussions to be easily discerned. When e-mailing, some students concentrated exclusively on the evidence they had identified without relating the specific tutorial topic to the broader question of its significance for understanding the Middle Ages. Others treated the two parts of the exercise quite separately, so that the e-mail contributions had less impact on tutorial discussions than we had originally hoped.

So, at the end of our second attempt to integrate e-mail into the first year history unit, we were still grappling with how to structure the exercise effectively. We had created a context that gave the students a reason for participating and successfully addressed student concerns so that we secured a high level of participation, but we had not quite managed to generate an extended e-mail debate that engaged students in the subject. It was back to the drawing board again.

How would you address this problem of student engagement?
What do you imagine happened next time around?

PART 3

The following year (the third iteration) we taught the first year survey of the Middle Ages as a single semester unit for the first time. This entailed some changes to the design and content of the course but it did not greatly affect the e-mail exercise. The course ran in the second semester so we were generally dealing with students who had settled into university study. Some were familiar with e-mail by the time they reached us but we continued to run workshops and provide support in the manner of the previous year. The e-mail debate was focused on the theme of the revised course, whether the early medieval period was deserving of the label 'the Dark Ages', and culminated again in a one-hour test paper. As in the previous year, e-mail contributions were to be made before meeting in tutorials and in class the students were still asked to identify an important piece of evidence to initiate discussion. There were three important changes:

1. We threw caution to the wind and set the e-mail debate as a compulsory part of the assessed work in the unit.
2. We required two 'responses' to other students' contribution. The contribution and responses were worth 15 per cent of assessed work.
3. Contributions were required on the significance of a set piece of reading relating to the tutorial topic. This piece of reading was intended to locate the specific tutorial issues in a broader historical context. Often it comprised a piece of primary evidence but sometimes we nominated a controversial interpretation relating to the tutorial topic.

These changes helped to facilitate greater interaction between e-mail contributions and tutorial discussion. The students explicitly related tutorial issues and readings to the nominated 'e-mail readings' when posting to the e-mail list, while aspects of the e-mail discussion were taken up in tutorials. Thus the discussions in each forum served to complement the other. The final test papers also suggested, once again, that the e-mail discussion list helped many students to make thematic connections between different issues and also to develop and clarify interpretations.

The new requirement that students 'respond' to other postings also helped to generate interaction. Nonetheless, the level of explicit debate among the students was still less than we had hoped, and much less that we had witnessed among later-year students. This led us to hypothesize that first year students are reluctant to engage directly with the ideas or arguments of others for fear of appearing critical or of being 'attacked' in return.

This hypothesis developed from student feedback during past years. In focus groups and surveys, students have often commented on how they felt 'intimidated' e-mailing faceless members of a discussion group. We have also observed that some students are uncomfortable disagreeing with others, sometimes because disagreement is regarded as an expression of hostility, and sometimes because they fear that their interpretation may then be 'wrong'. Some students may regard an invitation to debate as an opportunity to exchange ideas, others perceiving it as an occasion for point scoring and aggression which will potentially lead to their humiliation.

CASE REPORTERS' DISCUSSION

There are interesting questions here about the way students perceive certain modes of communication, learn new kinds of discourse and hone study and organizational habits as they progress through their university studies. Likewise these issues pose important challenges for academics' conceptions of their teaching roles and how universities go about meeting their responsibilities. They also raise questions about how realistic it is to expect first year students (predominantly school leavers), often engaging with e-mail technology for the first time, instantly to develop the self-confidence to enthusiastically embrace it and pursue a culture of openness and exchange for the purpose of developing their ideas, all within a 6- to 12-month time frame. For example:

- Is it practical to set up the required support structures and mechanisms to meet individual students' development needs under these sorts of conditions?
- To what extent do junior academics embarking on new careers have an adequate background to engage in such endeavours?
- Is it appropriate that universities expect them to tackle such challenges so early in their career?
- Are academic development units adequately equipped and appropriately oriented to advise on such matters?

I was glad to have got wind of Stephanie and John's formative plans at an early stage. This meant I was able to offer support and collaborate with them from the outset of this multi-year project. This collaboration was to pose its own challenges for me, however, since my own earlier experiences as a teacher-innovator (eg Trevitt *et al*, 1997) as well as my understanding from the literature (eg Loacker, Cromwell and O'Brien, 1986) suggested strongly that success would require the e-mail discussion activities to be built into the assessment structure. From the outset I was strongly of the opinion this was a necessary requirement if integration into the overarching learning design was going to be achieved.

On the other hand I not only respected Stephanie's strong desire to seek advice from the students, but also her desire to both act and be seen to act in accord with that advice. Thus, in the end, this meant that the trial went ahead as described even though I anticipated this would 'cost' us one development iteration (ie a year) while Stephanie and John came to the conclusion that integrating the discussion activities into the assessment structure would be the way to go. Of course, there was always the nagging doubt that I may be entirely wrong, and that something about their context (different discipline, different student cohort, etc) might mean that we would find ways to engage students without the compulsion of assessment. The gamble I had to take was that Stephanie's desire to persist and find a way to overcome challenges would prevail, even in the event that initial outcomes were discouraging. I had to have confidence that Stephanie would continue with the 'experiment' for at least two iterations by which time some positive outcomes should be forthcoming.

As mentioned, our end-of-course student surveys repeatedly revealed two overriding themes dominating student concerns. Technical issues and access to computers prevailed at the pragmatic 'frustrations' level. These themes are increasingly common for many universities in different countries, as indicated by recurrent discussion on the special interest American Association of Higher Education e-mail list run by Steve Gilbert (see www.tltgroup.org/). More deep-seated concerns were associated with student anxiety about 'going public' with incomplete ideas. These issues and concerns reflect and reinforce those revealed during earlier initiatives (eg Harasim, 1989) as well as contemporary developments (eg Johnson, Sutton and Poon, 2000) focused on technologically mediated student communications.

Finding ways to better support and assist students prepare for engaging in electronic 'public debate' is just one more example of the many contemporary challenges facing universities seeking to find and prove ways to more explicitly foster the development in their graduates of valued generic and transferable skills.

References

Harasim, L (1989) 'Online education: a new domain', in R Mason and A Kaye (eds), *Mindweave: Communication, computers and distance education*, pp 50–57, Pergamon Press, Oxford (www-icdl.open.ac.uk/mindweave/chap4.html)

Johnson, D, Sutton, P and Poon, J (2000) 'Face-to-face vs CMC: student communication in a technologically rich learning environment', in R Sims, M O'Reilly and S Sawkins (eds), *Learning to Choose: Choosing to learn*, Proceedings of the 17th annual ASCILITE Conference, Southern Cross University Press, Lismore, NSW

Loacker, G, Cromwell, L and O'Brien, K (1986) 'Assessment in higher education: to serve the learner', in C Adelman (ed), *Assessment in American Higher Education: Issues and contexts*, pp 47–62, Report no. OR 86–301, Office of Educational Research and Improvement, US Department of Education, Washington, DC

Trevitt, A C F, Åkerlind, G S, Brack, C L and Pettigrove, M (1997) 'The role of student assessment: To gauge students' performance, to enhance learning and professional skills, or to inform program evaluation?', in G Ryan (ed), *Learner Assessment and Program Evolution in Problem Based Learning: A monograph*, pp 33–50, Australian Problem Based Learning Network, The University of Newcastle, Australia

CHAPTER 8

CREDIT WHERE IT'S DUE

Case reporter: Robin Goodfellow

Issues raised

This case raises issues concerning the assessment of students' contributions to online collaborative learning, specifically when tutors attempt to apply criteria that had not been adequately specified in the course literature.

Background

The case concerns an online MA in Educational Technology, offered by a distance teaching university in the UK. The programme consisted of three courses each lasting 30 weeks. Although the courses were based in the UK, students took them from countries all round the world – logging on to the course Web sites and carrying out text-based discussion and collaborative learning tasks via a computer conference. The situation described here arose during the 1999–2000 presentation of the course, 'Information Technology in Distance Education', on which there were 50 students, mainly teachers and trainers from universities and companies based in 27 different countries. They were taught in groups of 10, each group working with a tutor who was either a full-time lecturer at the university, or a part-time 'associate lecturer' based elsewhere in the country (and in one case in another European country). The course had been authored by academics in the Educational Technology department, and was directed by the case reporter, who was responsible for coordinating the tutors and providing pedagogical leadership, as well as dealing with students on a one-to-one basis over matters of course organization and administration.

PART 1

I had been working in educational technology in UK universities for 10 years. This was my first experience, however, of running a global online course. The five tutors ranged in age from late 20s to mid-50s – their experience of teaching such a course was limited too, but two of them had graduated from the programme themselves, so they knew something about the student experience. The problem we all faced was that, despite a lot of consideration, we still did not know how to assess our students' contribution to online collaborative discussion. The university assessment process required students to submit individual written assignments for marking by the tutors. But having placed considerable emphasis on collaboration in the learning process the course team wanted to award credit for that too, to assess and reward students making the kind of commitment signalled as a key objective. Applying what we perceived as an innovative teaching approach, we did not want to end up marking assignments purely on conventional criteria of academic achievement.

The course had been built around learning activities that were intended to enable credit to be awarded to individuals while at the same time making that credit reflect their contribution to collaborative goals. For example, students were required to conduct an online debate over a two-week period. The tutors assigned roles – the conventional ones of proposer and opposer, plus more course-specific ones such as 'documentalist' (responsible for finding Web-based resources relevant to the debate topic), 'rapporteur' (responsible for reporting on the progress of the debate in other groups), and 'moderator' (responsible for managing the online group and seeing the task through to its conclusion). At the end of the two-week period the students were asked to reflect on the discussion and to write an essay presenting the main issues in the debate.

The conferencing software maintained a record of discussion, which meant that tutors could retrospectively evaluate individual students' contribution to the debate, as part of the overall assessment. Having individual contributions assessed meant that students would take the online discussion part of the course seriously (equivalent, in the face-to-face context, to insisting that they attend classes), and it also offered a way to evaluate their success in developing the required skills and attitudes. The course guide summed it up: '(You will be marked on...) your use of messages from the online debate to support your view. You are asked to include at least five messages of your own, as well as quoting from and commenting on key points (30%)'. The system seemed simple, appropriate and fair. As a team we were happy with it. What could possibly go wrong?

Once the course was under way, all went pretty smoothly for a while. I observed that all the students made some contribution to the debate, although the extent and quality of their individual contributions varied widely. However, when the first assignment became due, students began to ask us for more detail about how they were supposed to present these 'five messages of your own' in order to gain their 30 per cent. They wanted to know if five was an absolute minimum or a rough guide, whether they had to quote entire messages or extracts, if they could include messages contributed to the plenary conference or to other tutorial groups as well as their own debate, and if they could include other people's messages. Some wanted to know *why* they had to incorporate messages in this way – simply as evidence of their activity, or in order to demonstrate how their thinking had developed?

I was worried, and so were other members of the tutor team. Some of these questions were much harder to answer than we had thought. Hurried e-mail discussions ensued. The tutors were now less sure about what exactly they were supposed to be giving credit for. Eventually we agreed that it was the spirit rather than the letter of the 'five messages' that was important, and that each tutor should negotiate his or her own interpretation of the criterion with his or her tutor group. I sent a message to the course plenary conference announcing that the 'five messages' rule was not an absolute requirement, but that:

> we put a lot of weight on the way that online discussion is used to make/ support points. This is very important to the overall approach of this course, with its emphasis on the use of technology to enable collaborative and constructive learning. We urge you all to take seriously the question of how you can systematically exploit the discussion that goes on in the course conferences – ie how you can 'add value' to it in the way you encapsulate the exchanges in the essay. It will continue to attract a significant proportion of the marks.

Not surprisingly, this did not quell the tide of discontent. From the ensuing online discussion, and from e-mail conversations between students and tutors, it became clear that the process of negotiation was simply raising more questions about what counted as quality in the students' contribution to the debate, and how this could be represented and referenced in the essay. While some students seemed content to regard the openness of the brief as an invitation to be creative in the way that they used the debate record, others wanted to be told exactly how they could gain the 30 per cent of marks, if it were not by simply referring to five messages they had contributed to the discussion. We were besieged by requests for further explanation of what it meant to 'exploit the discussion' or 'add value' to it.

The problem for the course team about providing such explanations was, unfortunately, that although we knew in principle what we wanted to give credit for, we lacked the experience to know what successful integration of reference to online discussion into the assignment would look like in practice. Until we saw what the students actually did in the essays we couldn't be sure how we were going to mark them! The negotiation continued inconclusively until the assignment deadline was up, and the students had to submit whatever they had managed to produce out of the uncertainty.

How should the tutors set about marking the essays?
What criteria would you use to judge the significance of each contribution made to the discussion?
What do you think happened next?

PART 2

When all the students had finally submitted their assignments for marking, it became obvious that they had adopted quite a wide variety of approaches to the task of integrating references to the online discussion group into the assignment. The most basic approach was to incorporate simple references to messages that the student had sent to the conference. For example: 'moderating an online class requires special skills, as I said in my message #213...', usually followed by a pasted-in quote from the message. Although this approach arguably met the letter of the assessment criteria, and while some of the messages referred to were well-written and useful contributions to the debate, it seemed that they did little to construct the essay itself as a reflection on a collaborative process.

A less introspective tactic was to cite other people's messages in support of a point being argued, as though these were authoritative sources, eg, 'western educational systems are based on competition (Ian K, message #257)...' However, unless such opinions were shown to be commonly held, or derived from the debate, as far as I was concerned they had no more weight than the writer's own and could not be accepted as adding anything to the knowledge construction process.

More promising were references to others' accounts of their personal experience: 'John describes tutoring his own online course, in message #234, and claims that the workload is greater for the online tutor...' In these cases a valuable experiential contribution was highlighted and drawn into the development of an argument. I considered that the students were showing both that they had appreciated the epistemological value of John's contribution and that they were prepared to build an element of their own understanding on the basis of it.

When some of the students went on to synthesize themes from the online discussion, I felt that indications of the real quality of their contribution started to become evident: 'coping with the information overload that was talked of in the audio cassette was a recurrent theme of our debate, sometimes as student reactions to the ongoing debate (messages #245, 345, 262)...' I thought that this kind of combination of knowledge of what was being talked about online, with understanding of the current experience that it was rooted in, was evidence of a deeper insight into the process of collaboration than that shown by merely quoting others' words. Interestingly, however, such reflection did not require the writers to have actually contributed to the discussion themselves, a realization which caused me to reconsider the value of counting the number of messages contributed by an individual and to revise my presumption that online 'lurking' (reading messages but not responding to them) necessarily undermines the construction of knowledge.

Where a student both contributed to and was able to analyse the processes of online collaboration, I felt that the indicators of quality were at their most convincing: 'after an initial salvo of messages proposing and opposing the motion the debate became rather unfocused as the group struggled to nail down what I called the "wonderful wideness" of this "global" motion (message #265)...'

This student had in fact contributed rather fewer messages to the debate than some others, but, as this reflection suggests, the contributions that she made were on two levels – developing the topic itself and raising the group awareness of the nature of the online discussion process. This approach was refined in the essay, with conclusions being carefully drawn and illustrated directly by reference to interventions in the debate by the group moderator. One further aspect of this student's approach was the use of live links from the assignment text to messages and message threads in the online conference (the assignment was marked on screen), thus creating a hypertext document enabling the marker to click from comment to illustration and back to reflection.

I thus had clear evidence of variation in the quality of student response to this part of the assignment, and also realized that the quality of reflection in the essay was complementary to the quality of the contribution to the debate. I decided to suggest that the tutors grade the essays, and award the 30 per cent, according to five criteria:

Criterion 1: student has referred to five messages (their own or others') (5 marks).
Criterion 2: the references are relevant to the argument and inherently justified (personal experience, insight, etc) (5 marks).
Criterion 3: student has explicitly attempted to identify themes in the discussion, rather than simply quoting individual message content (5 marks).
Criterion 4: student has discussed the process by which these messages were generated, rather than focusing only on the topic (10 marks).
Criterion 5: student has used the hypertextual capabilities of the electronic medium to physically integrate the essay and the debate record (5 marks).

When the marking was finished and the assignments had been returned to the students, with comments from the tutors, I posted a message to the plenary conference explaining the criteria and arguing that, although they had not been stated beforehand, they were logical and fair, and could be said to be heavily implied in the focus in the course literature and subsequent discussion on 'key points' and 'encapsulating exchanges'.

Rather than settling the issue, this sparked a debate that lasted for the next two weeks. Some students objected to the retrospective publishing of assessment criteria, and complained that they could not possibly have worked out these criteria for themselves. I countered by arguing that as they were engaged in an explicit knowledge-construction process, the tutors could not possibly have known in advance what knowledge would be created and therefore any criteria they could have published would have necessarily been too general to be useful. Privately I felt that, looked at from the point of view of openness, these students had a point. They had been used rather as guinea pigs in what turned out to be an experimental approach. On the other hand, as a tutor group we had little doubt that the marks eventually awarded fairly reflected the relative constructiveness of individuals' involvement in the activity. The dispute settled down after the students who had received the best marks agreed to publish their essays on the conference, for all to see and learn from. I chose to regard the whole episode as itself part of a collaborative investigation into virtual learning.

What is your reaction to Robin's approach?
Do you think the students were treated fairly?
Are there any consequences from this case for your own teaching?

CASE REPORTER'S DISCUSSION

There is no doubt that, as a course team, we broke one of the golden rules of openness in distance education: that criteria for assessment should be made explicit in advance. On the other hand, with computer-mediated communication enabling a high level of interaction between students and the course team, it could be argued that this was a case of genuine negotiation of the terms of assessment, as part of the learning process for tutors as well as students. The course team in this case felt justified in claiming the latter, for two principle reasons. First, the issue of how to assess the online discussion was clearly relevant to this particular area of study – educational technology. As the students were studying the use of media in learning and teaching by using it themselves, there was a sense that they were already their own guinea pigs. The more perceptive of the students obviously realized this and accepted the whole assessment issue as a learning opportunity. This is clearly not a justification that could be used in subject areas where the role of technology in the learning process is not itself part of the content (art history, or geology, for example).

Second, the students in this case were at postgraduate level, professionally experienced and arguably more intrinsically motivated, less affected by the ultimate grade and more likely to look for value in the process itself. Such students are usually capable of negotiating learning processes and outcomes, enabling teachers to adopt a non-authoritative, facilitating role, even to the extent of becoming co-learners. There is much literature on the subject (see for example Harasim, 1995) and most of it is in agreement that the passing of responsibility for learning from the teacher to the student is one of the characteristics of progressive pedagogy in general and online educational innovation in particular. Virtual learning environments do seem to alter familiar teacher–student and student–student relations, as many of the usual trappings of status and expertise are absent. However, this has implications for formal systems of assessment, which need to reflect this democratization. Furthermore, there is no guarantee that all students who come to online learning, for whatever reason, will be ready for such autonomy. Those who are still teacher dependent and grade oriented may lose their way in environments in which collaboration with other learners, and negotiation with teachers, is regarded as integral to the learning outcome.

Despite the virtuality of the learning environment, and the digital nature of the discussions, the key issues underlying the difficulties experienced by the team should be familiar to anyone who has been involved in education for credit. There is the question of whether it is process or product that is being assessed – giving marks for an essay (product) on the basis of how well it reflects on a discussion (process) is not the same as giving marks for the discussion itself. If the institutional policy on assessment rules out collaborative marking of discussion work, as it did in this case, then it is only the reflective essay that can actually be assessed, however important the discussion is considered to be. We needed to make this clear, and also to make clear the kind of knowledge and skills required for successful constructive reflection in this subject area, and to ensure that the students were helped to develop these. Where students were not accustomed to reflective writing they should have been given examples of good practice. Conventions for referencing messages should have been discussed in advance. And since the medium of interaction itself influenced the process of reflection, by making textual evidence constantly and instantly available, the students needed to be shown explicitly the technical possibilities and limitations.

There is also the reliability of the marking process itself. How is it possible to ensure that comparable assignments will receive comparable marks? The course team were committed to a constructivist teaching approach, and to the principle of negotiation between students and tutors over the interpretation of marking criteria, but we ended up with the tutors arguing among ourselves. The way to prevent this was to have started from some point of agreement among the tutors about what counted as success and failure in terms of the objectives of the course overall. Only when we were happy that we would at least all recognize a distinction-level essay when we met it, should we have attempted to publicly reinterpret the criteria that the course authors had set.

Finally there is the question of how problems in the assessment process can be dealt with in subsequent presentations, without radically changing the nature of the course. The department was very keen that lessons learnt in one course should be propagated to the others, and that the university's standard tutor-monitoring procedures should be supplemented where possible by course-specific approaches to the kinds of issue discussed here. It was decided to establish a special tutor conference in the weeks leading up to the beginning of the next course, in which the tutors could discuss some essays from the previous course, and select three to be made available to the students as models of how to integrate reference to online collaborative discussion. The record of the previous year's online discussion would also be available, and the criteria for awarding 30 per cent for online contribution that I had worked out would be used as a focus for discussion of the relation between collaborative work and the course objectives. Before the course started each tutor would be expected to publish his or her own version of these criteria on the conference, for criticism by the others. In this way it was expected that the principle of negotiating the meaning of credit-for-collaboration with the students could be preserved, and indeed practised, without jeopardizing the validity or reliability of the assessment process.

Reference

Harasim, L (1995) *Learning Networks. A field guide to teaching and learning online*, MIT, Cambridge, MA

CHAPTER 9

It SEEMED LIKE A GOOD IDEA AT THE TIME

Case reporter: Ron Oliver

Issues raised

The main issue raised in this case concerns the unexpected and perverse outcomes that can develop when a seemingly positive change is introduced to a course. The need for monitoring to pick up unexpected developments is crucial.

Background

This case study takes place in the Faculty of Communications and Science at an Australian university, in a unit entitled Communications Networks. The teacher is a 40-year-old male and the subject is a second year core unit in a graduate diploma multimedia course. The course has been designed by the teacher and is supported extensively through the use of Web-based resources and learning materials. For the unit, in 1997, the lecturer had developed an innovative set of Web-based learning activities involving the use of student-centred inquiry and bulletin board postings. The learners all have sound computing skills and access to the World Wide Web through their own personal computers, university computers or computers at their work sites.

PART 1

The unit that I was teaching was all about the new communications technologies and from one semester to the next it was very difficult to keep the course content current, given the dynamic nature of the field. We were using a very good textbook that provided strong examples and descriptions of the various technologies underpinning the field, but it was not current in terms of its examples and applications. In fact the textbook was in its fifth version and still needed to be updated. Although it provided a good framework and theoretical structure for the course it needed to be supplemented by more recent materials and examples, and the Web proved to be the perfect supplementary source of information for the course. On the Web there was an unlimited amount of material describing current developments in communications technologies, all of which was easily accessible to the learners.

As course coordinator, I endeavoured to keep abreast of the material available on the Web and spent a considerable amount of time each week searching for information and updating the course Web pages to include new links to the sites that I found. Of course I also needed to spend time removing outdated links – another time-consuming task for the developer of Web-based learning materials.

The teaching format that I had been using in this class was to have all students prepare for the weekly lecture by completing a series of pre-readings and written activities based on this material. As preparation for each weekly lecture, students were given an open-ended inquiry task to explore. The task attempted to take students beyond the content of the textbook and to contextualize the topic into some meaningful authentic situation. Often the task required students to apply the knowledge in some way to suggest a solution to a problem. The weekly lecture took the form of a summary of the content and included a degree of learner interactivity. As I discussed the content and the various applications, I encouraged students to contribute to the general discussion based on their reading and inquiry. Having the students familiar with the topic through their preparatory reading helped to make these sessions lively and informative with input from many of them adding to the discussion and topic development.

Previous experience had shown me that the students needed to be encouraged to do the lecture preparation activities. To motivate them to prepare, I allocated marks each week on the basis of their preparation. The students were marked on the extent of their answers to the questions and their responses to the weekly problem, and a component of their overall assessment was the cumulative mark of the weekly activities. This learning environment worked very well and the students were quite positive in their feedback about the quality of the learning experiences and their overall levels of satisfaction with the process.

The next semester I added a new component to the course. I realized that I was never going to keep up with the Web and the links for this course so I decided to have the students help me, and developed a simple Web tool by which students could post useful URLs to a bulletin board.

I added this tool to the course Home Page and made it a requirement for all students as part of their weekly activities to locate and post at least one useful URL to the bulletin board. My idea was that this activity would have all my students scouring the Web for useful links for the course and, through the posting activity, they could share their findings with others in the class. Better yet, the large number of links that would be posted for each topic provided me with an instant set of useful links for the next semester. The idea was quite simple but appeared to hold many benefits for both the students and me.

To encourage student participation, I allocated some of the weekly marks to the quality of the site that was posted and students could post one good site or several reasonably good sites to get their full set of marks. I also used to take a few chocolate bars into my lectures each week and would hand these out to the students who found the best sites. We used to call the best site the 'choccy site of the week' and competition was fierce.

What problems do you anticipate might arise with this arrangement?
Would you do anything before starting?

PART 2

The use of the URL posting appeared to be running quite smoothly. The bulletin board was replete each week with wonderful sites and the students really appeared to be enjoying the process and indicated that they found value in using those posted by the other students as part of the research activity. But then I noticed some interesting trends:

- the first URLs for each week always seemed to be coming from the same students;
- students started posting the URLs very early in the week, sometimes more than one week ahead (when they should have been exploring the previous topic);
- a number of students stopped posting URLs altogether; and
- several students dropped out of the course without any word as to why.

These things together caused me to stop and reflect and I started to look around to see what was happening in the class. I spoke to several of the students and discovered some unexpected issues. Many students were not happy at all with the process and reported the following problems.

Finding good sites on the Web was relatively easy if you were one of the first students to attempt the task. All it took was a search with a relatively simple keyword, for example the weekly topic, and the search engine would return some very useful links. It was interesting to note that most students used the same keywords and the same search engines, which often saw them finding the same sites that others had already posted. Then it was back to the drawing board to find more.

The Web might contain a wealth of information but there are many impediments to locating it. The students reported many frustrations even among relatively simple searching tasks. Such problems as network failures, disconnections, untimely delays and large download times were common even for those using the high-speed networks at the university.

The students tended to use quite simple search strings that returned large numbers of hits, all of which had to be screened to find ones that were relevant. They reported that this took many attempts and often the majority of sites they inspected were irrelevant and unsuitable for their needs. Sifting through the myriad of sites was time consuming and often fruitless.

The part-time students reported many more difficulties than those studying full time. The part-time students had less flexibility in when they were able to do their inquiry and by the time they commenced their tasks, the best sites were often taken by others. Despite the vast amount of information to be gained from the Web, there was a high overhead in time needed to be successful.

Many students commented that they learnt very little from the sites that they found. They indicated that the bulk of their time was spent locating the information and then they were happy to post the URL and often made little use of the information in their inquiry. This was a case of the activity being an end in itself rather than a means to an end, as I had planned. When asked if they had used any of the sites posted by others, they tended to answer 'No'. There was lots of information available but not much use was being made of it.

The signs were obvious. My neat solution to the problem of keeping the site contents up to date was falling apart and students were feeling frustrated about the whole exercise. What had started out as a creative innovation was turning into a burden.

Why had this situation developed?
What options were available to the teacher at this stage?
What would you have done?

PART 3

My solution was relatively simple. I removed the compulsion associated with posting sites and told students that they should only post sites if and when they found something worth sharing. The outcome from this small change was twofold: a reduction in the number of sites posted accompanied by an associated increase in time being spent attending to the information available and the inquiry tasks themselves. The students were much happier with this and we continued through the semester in a much more learning-focused and task-oriented fashion.

How well was this situation handled?
Does this case highlight any issues for your own teaching?

CASE REPORTER'S DISCUSSION

This case highlights the unexpected twists and turns that the introduction of a seemingly progressive and 'neat' solution can take. It also highlights the need to closely monitor how a course is going so as to find out about unintended and undesirable directions.

For many years I had been planning and delivering a range of innovative learning activities to students studying face to face and I had been accustomed to receiving feedback and input from them in direct and meaningful ways. The move to the online environment had altered the lines of communication, and in the online mode I did not receive the cues from the learners as I had before and so their difficulties may have remained undetected for a longer time.

In terms of monitoring the activities of the online learners, I was amazed at the number of different ways in which they attempted the same tasks and equally amazed at the number of different outcomes achieved. It became apparent to me that it is not possible, nor wise, to use one's expectations and anticipations as the basis for deciding the success of a project. With online learning, there is a real need for the teacher to closely monitor learners' activities and responses to ensure that they are in accord with what is expected and required. There are so many things to go wrong and so many things that can impede online learning, that teachers need to be ever vigilant to discover what these are and what new ones have emerged since the last one was rectified.

Another issue that emerged from this incident was the need to negotiate with learners to ensure that they are happy with the tasks they have been set. I was surprised to find that my URL posting activity, despite its potential, was seen as a burden by some of the learners. Now when I introduce learners to new activities, I indicate that they have the capacity to choose to participate and any who are not comfortable with the environments that I set can negotiate with me to find some more accommodating process.

It goes without saying that it can be administratively 'heavy' to have to deal with large numbers of students wanting to negotiate 'individual classroom agreements' and knowing this, I tend to try to encourage learners to 'have a go' when they are first confronted by an environment that they think they will not enjoy. I find that if I can get students to come with an open mind and if I monitor the process closely, there are very few who do not prefer the learning activities associated with contemporary online learning environments. Often it is the change from a teacher-directed setting to a more student-centred one that causes the most alarm. But after a few sessions in settings where they are well supported by resources, learning heuristics and scaffolds for their learning, most learners come quickly to appreciate and value the changed style of learning. Sometimes they have to be convinced, but then the sign of a good teacher is the ability to lead and motivate learners to take responsibility for their own learning and to value the outcomes that are achieved.

A final issue to emerge from this incident concerns the manner in which assessment can be used as an inducement for student participation. Assessment is perhaps the strongest motivating force a teacher can use to encourage students to complete activities, and it is of course a strategy used by many teachers. When assessment is used in this way students will participate, but as this case demonstrates, from a learning perspective, allocating marks for participation alone is not really a valid strategy. In other settings some teachers allocate marks to induce students to contribute to chat rooms and bulletin boards. However, this incident gave me a clear sign that making these sorts of activities compulsory and assessing participation without consideration of the quality of the participation, is inappropriate. Assessment needs to reflect achievement of learning outcomes and if it is to be used as an inducement for Web-based learning, it needs to be applied in a fashion where it does actually involve some measure of learning. In this instance I really needed to allocate marks on the basis of the quality of the URL provided and perhaps the extent to which this was expressed in the summary provided by the learner.

As with most forms of human activity, learning and advancement are achieved when the activity is undertaken in a reflective and thoughtful fashion. This incident provided many hints and tips to guide my teaching practice, and subsequent implementations of this learning activity have been undertaken with modifications and changes based on the feedback received and discussed above. But each new implementation creates new settings and provides many more unexpected instances, each of which serves yet again to provide information that continues to inform and guide my teaching practice.

The episodes mentioned in this case study happened quite early in my adoption of Web-based teaching strategies and the memories have lived with me. Since this time I have implemented a range of different learning strategies in my classes but have been careful in each instance to be aware and understand the potential impacts that the new ideas can have on individual learners. I now undertake any new idea with a sense of caution and try to imagine the many different impacts and influences that could arise. I think of the many different types of learners I have, their different predispositions to learning, their different personal aims, their different opportunities and the different ways in which they approach their studies. Now I know that any innovation will return at least a dozen variations in form when implemented and I actively look to see which forms support learning and which don't.

The technologies themselves provide strong conduits for the forms of information interchange needed to keep in close contact with the learners. I use Web-based feedback forms, bulletin boards and e-mail to stay close to the feelings and impressions of the learners. I am attentive to their levels of participation in activities and provide encouragement in instances where participation has waned. More often than not the encouragement is aimed towards the larger cohort than the individual learner, but its presence is driven by feedback from individuals. Each semester sees a raft of variations being made to the learning strategies I use and each semester new problems emerge. This evolutionary process appears as though it can and will go on forever and represents what I think is one of the more interesting and engaging aspects of using Web-based teaching. Everything changes, nothing stays the same and there is still so much to explore and do. And next year, there will be new technologies, new opportunities and students whose needs still remain to be met.

PLANNING AND DEVELOPMENT ISSUES

CHAPTER 10

OF HEAVEN AND HELL

Case reporters: Leonie Rowan and Chris Bigum

Issues raised

This case explores issues associated with the use of videoconferencing technology in university teaching. It discusses a model for planning the use of technology and for reflecting upon the consequences of incorporating technologies into teaching situations.

Background

The two reporters of this case work in the Faculty of Education and Creative Arts at Central Queensland University (CQU) in Australia. CQU's largest campus is in Rockhampton, but there are four significant 'branch' campuses located between 100 and 400 kilometres away from this site. The case explores decisions that were taken regarding the use of videoconference technology to deliver a second year, Bachelor of Education subject entitled 'Gender as a Social Justice Issue' to students located on a different campus to their lecturer.

PART 1

Since 1994 the Faculty of Education and Creative Arts at CQU has offered the first year of its Bachelor of Education at the main campus and three satellite campuses: Bundaberg, Gladstone and Mackay. Prior to 1997, it was expected that after completing their first year, students at the branch campuses would relocate to Rockhampton to finish their degree. In 1997, the university's faculties were strongly encouraged to extend their offerings on the satellite campuses. For our faculty this meant that three more years of the Bachelor of Education had to be phased in to these sites.

There were serious challenges here. The majority of faculty staff were located in Rockhampton and there were no funds available for new staff to be appointed to the satellite campuses. Staff were encouraged to make use of newly installed videoconferencing technology to address the problem.

In this context Leonie (based in Rockhampton) was asked to teach a second year subject entitled 'Gender as a Social Justice Issue' to students in Bundaberg (350 kilometres away). For some years prior to this Leonie had taught a first year subject to all four campuses using videoconference technology. Because of this the expectation within the faculty was that she would be able to use the same technology to teach this new unit.

From her experiences Leonie was well aware that she was facing considerable challenges. She recognized that while videoconferencing technology – telephone calls with pictures – allows for the real-time transmission of images and sound and brings staff and students separated by distance into a shared (virtual) classroom, it has limitations. At the transmission speeds provided by the university network, picture quality is far from perfect. The image breaks up slightly when people move and it is difficult to see facial expressions or gestures. Speech and lip movement are not well synchronized and it can be hard to determine who is speaking at any particular time. Audio levels and clarity can vary unaccountably and 'feedback' between sites can mean that a lecturer hears an echo of his or her voice when speaking. The technology also has a disconcerting habit of crashing. The line can drop out or the image can freeze necessitating a disconnection and reconnection. In most cases, these problems can be addressed only by technical support staff (who are not always on standby outside the videoconference room!) which means considerable time within any lesson can be lost.

The subject matter involved for this particular subject – gender as a social justice issue – provided another set of challenges. Even in their mildest forms, discussions around gender generally require individuals to reflect upon their own beliefs, their life choices, and their relationships with and attitudes towards others. In the case of the unit Leonie was teaching, students were encouraged to think about the impact that gender has had upon students in various educational contexts, and the ways in which they, as future teachers, could respond to gender-related challenges.

From her experiences in face-to-face gender classes Leonie was aware of the time and effort it takes to foster debate without alienating the students. Keeping things on an even keel depends upon a lecturer's ability to establish rapport with students and demonstrate that he or she values and respects their personal opinions. If the lecturer isn't also the tutor, then the role of the tutor becomes crucial.

With these issues in mind Leonie decided that she needed to plan very carefully indeed how she was going to deal with the subject and the technology. It was at this time that she became aware of the work of one of her colleagues with a form of educational planning known as 'scenario planning'. Chris had been interested in scenario work for a number of years and had used it in distance teaching and planning with a range of educators and groups. His approach was based on the work of the Global Business Network (www.gbn.org).

Scenario planning has the same purpose as teaching: to shift the mindsets of participants. Chris had found the best way to demonstrate the power of scenario planning was by doing it. He offered to walk Leonie through the process addressing the question: how will the subject 'Gender as a Social Justice Issue' be received by the students in Bundaberg?

The process has a number of stages. First, Leonie had to identify all of the influences that she thought could impact on the problem. She came up with such things as the size of the student group, their prior experiences, her own preparation, the role of the tutor, the support from other staff, library resources, student access to additional study materials, and the technology itself.

Chris then had Leonie classify each influence as either predictable or uncertain. She was certain, for example, that the student group would be small but she was uncertain about the reliability of the technology. She was then asked to reduce her list of uncertainties to two using the criteria that they were, in her view, the least certain *and also* the most important in terms of her question. Leonie identified the role of the tutor (who she had not yet employed) and the stability of the technology as the critical uncertainties she was faced with. The next step was to agree on how to operationalize each uncertainty: to think about the probable, extreme states that each uncertainty could be in.

In Leonie's experience, the role of the tutor (in terms of the students' acceptance of the subject overall) had two possible extremes: the tutor could be either rejected or accepted by the students. In the case of the technology the two most plausible extremes were that the technology would work well allowing for regular, uninterrupted links between herself and the students, or it could be unreliable in terms of the stability and quality of connection. Using each uncertainty as an axis, Chris drew an X–Y grid for the four scenarios; this is shown in Figure 10.1.

Scenario planning requires the participants to take the time to think about what each situation – each possible scenario – would actually be like. A key part of this process is giving each scenario a name or generating a new lexicon with which to think and talk about the problem. Leonie's already high level of anxiety about teaching the subject made naming Scenario 3 pretty simple. Here was a case in which she did not have reliable access to the students who were also alienated from their tutor. In this scenario the tutor was demanding, unsympathetic and anxious for the students to demonstrate sophisticated skills of analysis. It was christened 'hell'.

From this beginning the labels for the other three scenarios flowed rela-tively easily. Scenario 1 was clearly a teacher's heaven. In this educational

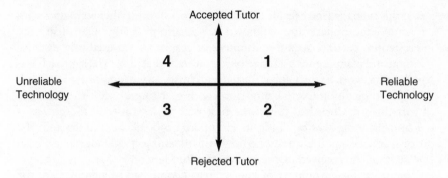

Figure 10.1   The scenario grid

Nirvana the technology allowed for a good exchange of ideas between Leonie and her students, and the tutor built upon issues explored in the interactive seminars in a supportive and empathetic manner. Students felt valued and appreciated, and achieved significant outcomes.

While heaven and hell were easy to identify it took Leonie and Chris some time before they were able to remember enough about their Catholic upbringing to label the other states. Eventually they found the names: Scenario 2 was not quite hell, but it was certainly an unpleasant state to be in: a real case of purgatory. Here the technology was reliable, but the work covered in the interactive seminars was consistently undermined by events in tutorials. The students became resentful of their tutor who asked too much of them, and began to avoid the subject.

Less stressful than purgatory but a long way from heaven, Scenario 4 became our limbo. Here the lecturer took comfort from the fact that the students were well looked after, and seemed happy with their tutor, but was frustrated by not being able to capitalize upon the positive work of the students and the tutor because of unreliable technology.

Out of this scenario activity, therefore, Leonie and Chris were able to identify four very distinct, and very plausible scenarios that could result through the course of teaching the subject. With these scenarios in mind, Leonie felt ready to deal with the course. She acknowledged that while teaching the subject was going to be challenging, it *could* have positive outcomes and that she would need certain strategies to respond to the situations that might develop. With a strong desire to make it to heaven, a willingness to spend some time in limbo and recognition that the roads to hell and purgatory were paved with technological inventions, she took several steps to prepare for the semester.

First, as a result of recognizing the pivotal role of the tutor, Leonie tried to find someone who possessed (as far as she could tell) not only the necessary discipline knowledge base but also sophisticated interpersonal skills. She then spent time 'training' the tutor: making explicit her desire for the tutor to act as a mediator between the students and the lecturer, between the students and the material, and between students and other students. From Leonie's perspective the emphasis was to be placed on the mindset shifts – however small or large – that occurred among the students, rather than on the acquisition of huge amounts of content knowledge. Leonie did not, however, provide concrete examples of what she expected from student assignments and did not share with the tutor her scenario planning activity for she was worried about the pressure this might place on that staff member.

With the tutor in place, Leonie moved to design the subject in such a way as to take maximum advantage of the videoconference technology and to minimize the effects of any disruptions. As a first step, she ensured that the videoconference session could operate as only one part of an overall teaching model. The students would also have access to a detailed study guide, a set of readings, their local tutor and a two-hour tutorial. The tutor would have copies of all lecture notes. The videoconference sessions were then designed to be interactive rather than didactic, in order to maximize student interest and enhance Leonie's ability to gauge student opinion.

During their first videoconference session Leonie explained that the sessions were to be sites for discussion and a sharing of ideas and emphasized the fact that she was looking for the students' willingness to think, rather than their ability to agree with what she said. Throughout each session Leonie spent as much time as possible engaging in conversation and seeking to demonstrate that there was not necessarily any 'right' answer to the questions and debates that were explored. She used a range of resources – videos and various documents that transmitted well via the document camera – invited in guest speakers and gave students the opportunity to make their own presentations.

The first six weeks were hell. Leonie asked herself: 'What on earth possessed me? How can things be going so wrong, when I planned so carefully? Why me?'

The specific causes of Leonie's anxiety were varied. The technology caused five disruptions to the first six videoconferences. The audio levels were poor and she conducted one session with her head almost on the desk (and closer to the microphone) in order to try and improve clarity. Guest speakers were not familiar with the technology and did not make the sessions interactive: they gave the students little chance to ask questions and appeared rather intimidating. In addition, the tutor appeared to be alienating the students extremely quickly, criticizing their understanding of the key debates and giving extremely low grades for early pieces of assessment.

Leonie started to get feedback via other staff at the campus, who were aware how closely she wanted the situation monitored. Students also sent e-mails directly to her, and occasionally called in for a face-to-face discussion if they happened to be in Rockhampton. While not everyone was unhappy, the students were clearly not in educational heaven. 'She hates us.' 'Why doesn't she listen?' 'Why can't we have a lecturer here?' These were the kinds of remarks that students in the videoconference classes began to make. They, too, felt themselves to be in hell.

What do you think Leonie actually did?
What do you think she should have done?
Has scenario planning helped so far? Can it help now?

PART 2

During the planning phase, Leonie was forced to think about the factors that could combine to generate each of the four scenarios, and the ways in which she could attempt to avoid them. She therefore understood the amount of work that was going to be necessary to try to control both the technology and the students' reactions.

The scenario activity also helped Leonie recognize how important it was to be prepared to respond to any of the four scenarios as/when they *did* develop. This meant she needed to have regular student feedback structured into the semester so she would actually *know* if she was on a descent into hell. When the feedback indicated above started to come through, instead of panicking or losing heart, she was prepared to implement a range of responses. Without this feedback it is doubtful that Leonie would have been able to gauge student reaction and she had little doubt that the final location would indeed have been hell.

As it was, Leonie was able to act quickly when it became clear that she was in trouble. She took several immediate steps. First, she modified the kind of contact she had with the tutor and instigated regular, detailed phone calls (something she had avoided initially because of the tutor's demanding schedule). She also began to provide detailed examples of the kind of feedback that it was appropriate to give students; she acted as a moderator for student assignments and visited the Bundaberg students to reassure them. She spent more time during the videoconference sessions discussing small and less controversial issues, and encouraging the students when they indicated a willingness to move into more detailed discussion.

Slowly the situation changed. The technology worked smoothly (for no apparent reason!), the students and the tutor appeared to have developed more of an appreciation of each other's feelings and needs, with the tutor sensitized to the fact that these were, after all, students for whom the subject matter was new and very challenging. The students made interesting and thought-provoking presentations within the videoconference sessions, and ended up, on average, with very good results.

By the end of the semester, therefore, Leonie felt that all the participants in the unit – the students, the tutor and herself – had made considerable progress, achieved significant outcomes, and learnt a lot about the ways in which a mediated heaven and hell can be attained.

CASE REPORTERS' DISCUSSION

The road to hell is paved with good intentions, and for this particular case, there was a very real risk that the 'good idea' of using videoconference technology to teach students at a distance would generate far more problems then it would solve. Ultimately, the course achieved its objectives and the evaluations conducted at the end of the term were largely positive.

This, of course, was achieved only after careful monitoring of a situation within which it would have been all too easy for the lecturer to plough ahead with a rigid and demanding 'lecture' schedule, and to miss the ominous signs of student dissent. The scenario activity that Chris and Leonie worked through was valuable for several reasons. During the planning phase of the unit, the scenario activity helped Leonie move beyond her anxiety and identify the most critical uncertainties that she was faced with and to consider the ways the tutor and the technology would interact. It gave her a language to describe what she was particularly concerned about and encouraged her to identify in precise terms what it was she would consider as desirable outcomes for the unit. Importantly, these were less ambitious than what she would have aimed for in a face-to-face class and she understood from the beginning that less could well be more.

At the end of the term, and having reflected upon the relationship between the subject's delivery and the scenario activity, Leonie and Chris identified several ways the scenarios could have been used even more efficiently in the unit design. If the tutor had been involved in the scenario activity (or briefed about what happened) this may have increased her understanding of Leonie's objectives. Leonie could also have spent time thinking about the ways in which the students and guest speakers would impact upon the technology and provided both groups with more training in the use of cameras, microphones and so on. Finally, while the scenario activities encouraged Leonie to be ready to identify and respond to hell and purgatory, she did not really anticipate the consequences that would arise if the class ended up in heaven. When the technology worked smoothly, and the students were keen, Leonie often felt that she was not well enough prepared with more challenging or extension activities. One student, for example, sent regular e-mails to Leonie asking for additional resources to read, or to discuss issues uncovered in assignment preparation.

Despite these limitations, however, the scenario activity allowed Leonie to reflect critically upon the impact that a particular technology could have on her overall teaching and to recognize that this impact would be influenced in unpredictable ways by other elements in the class. In a university context where the addition of technology is often read unproblematically as evidence of quality teaching, the scenario work helped Leonie articulate some of the situations within which technologies can make teaching much harder work than would otherwise have been the case. This did not mean that the technology needed to be abandoned. Instead, the scenario work allowed Leonie to identify as clearly as she could in advance what could go wrong, and hence how she could respond if it did.

In sum, building the scenarios made us think beyond single 'what if' questions such as, 'What if the videoconference technology proves seriously unreliable?' to detailed imaginings of unanticipated situations like purgatory and limbo. In doing this we were able to rehearse teaching situations in addition to those we regarded as the best and worst case. We came to think about teaching more in terms of a *negotiation* involving complex assemblages of people, resources and technologies and trying to get them to work together.

Could scenario planning be used to help you plan the incorporation of technologies into your own teaching?
What are the critical uncertainties that relate to the technologies you use? How prepared are you to respond to each possible outcome?

CHAPTER 11

FROM MOULDY DISKS TO ONLINE FIX

Case reporters: Vikki Ravaga, Jennifer Evans, Taaloga Faasalaina and Jo Osborne

Issues raised

This case study concerns the upgrading and updating of a course and the challenges this poses to all areas (eg technology, software, hardware, textbook, course book, practical manual, assessment and staff support skills) when *any* area of a course is upgraded. It highlights and illustrates the need for careful planning and monitoring in a complex teaching and learning environment.

Background

The University of the South Pacific (USP) includes 12 nations spread across thousands of islands. USP has developed as a dual-mode institution with face-to-face teaching located at campuses in Fiji, Vanuatu and Samoa and teams at these sites also developing distance education materials. These materials are delivered through centres, located in each of the 12 member countries, which service a total of about 5,000 off-campus students.

The case involves the offering and ongoing development of an introductory Computer Studies course, CS121. First offered in 1993, the course was adapted from an externally purchased programme comprising videos, textbook, study plan and floppy disks. Vikki, who is the case reporter, was an instructional designer who began the revision of the course in 1996, when just 59 students were enrolled. The course, under the guidance of a team of academics and support staff, has experienced rapidly growing enrolment numbers since then.

PART 1

When I was assigned as the instructional designer and course team leader to revise the off-campus offering of CS121, this was an introductory computer course at degree level. It was based on WordPerfect, Lotus and Dbase 3+ for DOS, paralleling on-campus teaching at the time it had been developed. It was the only USP course offered at a distance that required compulsory use of computers. Student demand had steadily increased throughout the USP region and so a decision was made to offer the course more widely.

The development of distance education courses is managed by the Distance Education Unit (DEU). The usual team structure for the course development consists of a course writer (usually a lecturer from one of USP's teaching departments), and an instructional designer (usually the team leader), editor, course development assistant and a text processor (all from DEU). Assistance with graphics and multimedia input (eg audio and video) is available from the USP media centre.

Each course offered at a distance has a course coordinator, usually from the relevant teaching department, who is responsible for running the course, including writing and marking assignments and exams, answering student queries and conducting extra tutorials if required. Often, and ideally, the course writer is the course coordinator, but this is not always the case.

To prepare myself for the first team meeting for the revised and expanded offering of CS121, and to gain some background information, I wanted to find out what previous students had thought of the course and what correspondence there had been regarding the initial development and offering. I had to review files and consult closely with Taaloga, who had been the instructional designer on earlier versions of the course.

Unfortunately, there were few course evaluation forms to review, but the majority of students' comments focused on the request to have the course upgraded in terms of its software and relevance. Software decisions first made prior to 1993 weren't going to last long! And this was important, because as well as fulfilling programme requirements, students needed the computer skills they would acquire for other courses and for employment.

The files threw up some important issues in the offering of CS121, particularly at the USP Centre level, such as:

- computer software/hardware was difficult to obtain and maintain (in a tropical climate disks were going mouldy, and manuals were constantly going missing!);
- the course was expensive to run;
- enrolments had to be limited due to computer access;
- local tutors for student support were necessary but hard to find;
- teaching materials were seen to be inappropriate to the USP context;

- there were questions about what should be assessed, and how, in this skills-based course (especially given the limited resources); and
- the development 'life' of the course was a continuing problem given the constant upgrades and changes to computer software and hardware.

Most alarming was the previous course coordinators' recommendation to cancel the course because they believed that a course in computing studies could not be taught at a distance! At the same time there were constant demands by regional students and other staff in the teaching department to revise the course urgently because of new software needs and to bring the course in line with the on-campus version.

Although technology itself might eventually offer its own solutions, at this stage we could not do anything online as there was no Internet access in most USP Centres. Given the resources in the South Pacific region, floppy disks would be as 'hi-tech' as we could go, and these grew mildew faster than traditional print. The course was definitely going to be a challenge if it went ahead at all!

What do you think are the major decisions to be made with regard to developing this course?
With no Internet access what could be done to keep course content up to date?
How do you think the course developers proceeded?

PART 2

The CS121 course team met and all the issues I had already seen in the files arose again. The teaching department wanted to revise the content of the course to address student needs in the region, and use Windows 95 as the software platform for MSOffice Professional 4.3 – Word, Excel and Access. Leaping already to my mind were the obvious questions: did the centres have the hardware and software to support the course and how often would it need to be revised to stay on top of software changes? Which department would pay for and carry out the upgrades? There was no complete inventory of computer facilities in the centres, so a short survey would have to be undertaken. Enrolments in CS121 would also have to be limited by the number of computers in each centre to provide adequate access for the practicals and skills components of the course. To help overcome some of the technical and student queries that regularly occurred during the teaching of the course, everyone agreed that a local tutor would be a necessity. Could such a person be found in each country – someone who was proficient in the use of the new software?

Because of these complex issues, CS121 varied quite a lot from the usual pattern of course development. For a start, the course team involved more people than usual. In addition to the course writer (a lecturer from the Maths and Computing Department), the acting head from the computing section of the department was involved, as well as a lecturer who was teaching the course on campus and had previously been the coordinator for the off-campus course. Development and delivery also involved unusually complex liaison with the regional USP Centres and staff, as well as having implications for USP's Information Technology Services. So the team had input from several sections of the university as development continued.

Over the next eight months the team worked to produce the revision of CS121 and address some of the issues that had appeared previously. Problems arose when the course writer resigned from USP one month prior to the start of the semester, but agreed to continue to work on the four outstanding units. At this point we hadn't included a textbook as the course writer wanted to keep costs down and tailor the course to suit the needs of the students in the region. Thus the course comprised a course book, practicals manual and disks. After completing the revision however, the remaining course team members felt that a textbook should definitely be considered next time around to provide suitable illustrations of hardware and concepts discussed in the course book and help to further explain or clarify content if students got into difficulty.

The 1997 offering went ahead with enrolments of 132 across 10 centres. This was a big jump from the 59 students enrolled in 1996. There was a wide variance in the availability and ability of the local tutors appointed at the centres, so the new course coordinator (a replacement lecturer, not involved in the development, who took over course delivery for on- and off-campus) held fortnightly audio tutorials over the satellite link for them, to provide additional guidance in the administration and tutoring of the course.

No sooner had the course started than the coordinator requested a revision before it was offered again as the 1997 version was already out of date! New computers bought for the centres arrived with MSOffice 97 already installed, and so the CS121 practicals manual needed amending to include this option. The older computers, of course, still had the older software. Also, because of the limited number of university computers, students who had computers at their place of work were encouraged to use them, and exact software standardization was becoming a real headache. As an interim measure the course coordinator distributed new instructions for the practicals manual to cater for this change. Floppy disks with assignment data had been provided for local tutors to load on centre computers – some of these had apparently contained viruses or, in some cases, no data!

We kept a close eye on the assessment for CS121 as there were conflicting ideas about what should be assessed and how. One member of the team, from the teaching department, insisted that the practical component of the course should be formally assessed through regular tests. This was difficult given that there were fewer computers than students and also that the local tutors had different levels of proficiency. As a compromise arrangement, the assessment was split, with theory being tested in a mid-semester test and final examination, and skills being assessed in the assignments, which made it easier to spread the hands-on use of computers. This issue had also surfaced back in 1993 and looked like it would continue to do so until we could come up with some means of 'skills testing' that was equitable across the region. There was no team consensus on what should be assessed and how, and so we would undoubtedly visit this issue again.

Planning began for the next revision of CS121 in July 1997. An upgrade in software to Windows 97 for all centres was needed so that the problems with different versions of software would be eliminated. Over the next couple of months, the course team met and continued working on the 1998 revision, but delays occurred with the rewriting of sections in the course book due to the course writer's heavy on-campus teaching load. The team then decided that the 1998 revision and software upgrade would have to be deferred to 1999. So, the course would be offered in 1998 as it was, apart from some updates to the practicals manual.

In 1999, with Taaloga as team leader once more, the revision of CS121 was completed and a textbook integrated into it (a decision supported by student feedback). The software was updated to the 1997 versions. On- and off-campus versions of the course now had comparable content and used the same textbook. Enrolments off-campus had increased again, to 201, and had a pass rate above 70 per cent. Despite all our difficulties the course was very much up and running, and successful.

Nevertheless, we realize that CS121 will have to be continually updated in terms of its content and software/hardware requirements. Incorporation of a textbook in fact compounded the problems, with a new edition due to be released shortly. We feel exhausted, and we wonder how long the Distance Education Unit will be prepared to provide this kind of input. Looking ahead, we are aware that international aid money had been set aside to upgrade USP's regional satellite communication system, including direct online access linking all regional USP Centres. We can see this could have a profound effect on the teaching process, and certainly hope it can help iron out some of the problems this course exemplifies.

How do you see this course developing in the future?
Have you experienced similar upgrading cycles; how did you cope with these?
What consequences does the need for planning and control of upgrading have for future projects you are thinking of undertaking?

CASE REPORTERS' DISCUSSION

This case highlights the way in which the rapid changes and advances taking place in IT have all sorts of implications for teaching in the area of the technology itself. It also illustrates how the upgrading of part of a course can have consequences for all or many other aspects of it.

Tertiary education institutions in the developing world, such as USP, have to operate with limited resources, in a situation where very few students own personal computers, and access and ownership of computers in the general populace is very limited. This is compounded by the most expensive telecommunications charges in the world and narrow Internet bandwidths that make using the Internet extremely slow and frustrating. We hear people from the United States and Europe talking with dismay about the 'world wide wait', but they have no idea of what 'waiting' means in the South Pacific.

Nevertheless people in this part of the world are just as curious about computers and as eager to become part of the Internet revolution as people anywhere else. Computers are widely used in business and commerce and although USP's small island states do not have large-scale work opportunities for many kinds of university graduates, there are jobs for those with skills and knowledge in computers. There have been persistent demands for training programmes in IT from students, governments, non-government organizations and the business community. These demands and the increasing student enrolments in CS121 were the impetus for the original offer and continued upgrading of the course. This was despite the very considerable obstacles that the course encountered in terms of expense, lack of local expertise, and limited availability of hardware and software.

Despite student demand, however, USP was operating in a context where the technology available to deliver the course lagged behind. The essential and major part of the course materials had to remain print based but the very nature of the course carried a technological imperative – students had to have access to computers that worked reasonably efficiently and had appropriate software programs. The conflicts that arose over assignments and assessment showed the significance of the practical, hands-on technology aspect of the course and the difficulty of evaluating students' achievements in this area compared with the somewhat easier task of teaching and assessing the theoretical aspect. From the pedagogical perspective it was recognized that theory and practice in this course could not reasonably be separated and one should be taught in conjunction with the other. However, technological and organizational limitations outweighed this concern, resulting in a false divide between the 'theoretical' components of the course (hardware configuration and function, etc) that were tested in exam situations but not practically applied, and practical skills acquisition which students demonstrated in assignments. Perhaps if there had been a greater focus on integrated assessment at an early stage in course development this might have generated some pragmatic and imaginative solutions. Instead the divided approach was allowed to develop and accepted as inevitable and insurmountable.

Organizational issues (hardware, software and staffing) are central to the case. These would not normally be the concern of the instructional designer or even staff from the teaching departments, who would not have authority over the running of the regional centres. However, all the 'telling' questions come up at the point of delivery and because of the course's unique needs it was often unclear who had responsibility and authority to act at this point.

Because of its particular geographic, economic, political and cultural context, USP faces enormous challenges in the intra-national delivery of its distance education programmes. The teaching of computer studies by distance education has been particularly problematic, as this case study shows. IT is changing and advancing so rapidly that it poses new teaching problems for all tertiary institutions worldwide. In the developing countries the ability to adjust flexibly, upgrade and update is especially difficult. Hardware/ software and course content have to be reviewed continually in order to remain usefully current. Such streamlining, driven by student demand, is not readily met within an institutional system unused to responding in this way, and often without the resources to do so.

The USP model for the production and offer of distance courses is a five-year cycle, which is obviously totally inadequate for a course dealing with IT. As we saw in the case study, the 1997 version of the course (that had been prepared in 1996) was out of date before it had started running. Apart from the ongoing cost of staff time and effort necessary to keep the course up to date, the costs of print materials for CS121 would be higher than usual because of the need to print small numbers of new materials for every single offer, and the wastage of any excess materials.

Future prospects look bright, however. Computers and communications technology are becoming cheaper and more widely available. More computers and a greater use of CD ROMs may provide some solutions to the problems of CS121, and there is the promise of finally getting online. In 2001 all regional centres are expected to have Internet access, plus e-mail, computer data transfer, fax and phone services. Audio teleconferencing, which has been used at some USP Centres since the 1970s, will finally become possible between all 12 countries of the region. In addition it is expected that some point-to-point videoconferencing will be available. A whole new world of technological potential will be opened. Hypothetically applied to the CS121 problems, for instance:

- better computer access in the centres would cater for an increase in enrolments and greatly improve assessment possibilities;
- online tutoring would diminish the regional variance currently experienced – and would be used to train local tutors; and

- online access to USP central servers would enable more reliable programme upgrades and two-way data transfer.

Dependence on an online fix, however, can only be justified by quality and reliability of the supply. Development still needs to be properly planned, designed and coordinated; and systems need to be monitored and evaluated. Although the technology may change appreciably, the 'upgrade' conundrum – that is, the effect of an upgrade in one area on many other areas – will remain a real dilemma.

Success at the USP lies in improving access to knowledge and skills for what must be some of the most remote and isolated students in the world, and who stand to benefit immensely from emerging information technologies if these can be made available. Questions about priorities of resource allocation, human and technological, are particularly pertinent when seen against the idiosyncrasies of the South Pacific situation. However, the extreme and unusual dimensions that this context brings to light in relation to teaching with technology may have valuable lessons for many other parts of the world, especially those where technology cannot be taken for granted and the possession of a personal computer remains an ambitious dream.

CHAPTER 12

'**I** HAVE SOME PAGES UP!'

Case reporters: Jo Bruce and Ruth Goodall

Issues raised

The case addresses the issue of the desirability of training academics on a one-to-one basis to create Web pages to support their teaching. It discusses how difficult it can be to reach academics using traditional training, and analyses a possible solution to the problem.

Background

The case takes place at the Centre for Staff and Educational Development (CSED) at the University of East Anglia. Jo is a sociology graduate with Web authoring skills developed at an Internet telecommunications company, and appointed as a Web officer in November 1998. It is envisaged that she will work on a one-to-one basis with lecturers to put up Web pages in support of their courses.

PART 1

It had been a bad week. First Emily Sargent had phoned to cancel her training session just 20 minutes before it was due to start, then John Peters had forgotten all about his and was not in his office when Jo called. To cap it all, in the middle of Sue's session she had received a phone call from her daughter to tell her that the water pipes in her house were leaking. As Sue had no way to get home the rest of the session was spent with Jo driving her there to deal with the problem. 'How on earth did I get myself into this?,' Jo ruefully asked herself.

She knew the answer, of course. At the end of 1998, within the university there was minimal and in some cases no support for Web page creation. We (Jo and other staff within the CSED) found ourselves working in an environment where the only option for putting pages on to the Web was for individuals to create them using HTML and later Web editing software.

So, if we were going to be training academic staff to be able to create and maintain their own Web pages in these circumstances we felt it was important to equip them with some key skills. We decided that the first skill would be to learn some basic HTML codes so they could gain a good understanding of the language they were to be using. Those of us working with the Web in the university had generally found that when people understand what they are working with they have a greater ability to fix things when they go wrong, as they invariably do!

Once they had some understanding of HTML, its possibilities, restrictions and potential, we could then introduce them to software that would enable them to create pages more easily. They could also look at other software to manipulate images for Web use and applications that could convert existing documents to Web pages.

We knew it was important to spend a significant proportion of the training working on real pages that the lecturers wanted to create. This was so they could achieve something by the end of the training and would have a set of pages to use as a model for anything else they wanted to put on to the Web. Another essential skill to equip people with would be how to design a Web site, taking into account layout, navigation and content issues. We felt that this should be dealt with throughout the training as a kind of evolutionary process.

Against this backdrop we introduced a training course of six/seven sessions each of two hours and encouraged lecturers to have at least a week gap between sessions. The training sessions covered a variety of issues depending on the skills of the individual, what they wanted to achieve and the computer they were running. The training was advertised through various means and individual lecturers contacted Jo directly to arrange sessions. Lecturers were encouraged to work between the sessions to progress and get the most benefit from the training.

We created a Web site to support the work, giving examples of sites that support teaching, had content suggestions and looked at some further techniques in creating sites. This is currently in the process of being updated so that all of the training available is on the Web. Participants can work through topics in their own time if they prefer.

Initial reactions and outcomes were very positive. We found that academic staff responded well and were keen to book on to the training. We had a high response rate compared to that for more traditional group training:

> The training was very flexible, rather than a standardized package delivered to everyone. We were able to tackle any issues/questions that arose. I've got a good grasp, have some pages up, a plan to work to and lots of ideas and enthusiasm.

An important ingredient of the Web training has been tailoring it to meet the needs and requirements of the individual lecturers. This way they are working on real rather than hypothetical issues and all the things they learn are relevant to what they want to do, so they see it as a better use of their time. One person wanted to create a virtual law library, rather than specific courseware, to support her students and colleagues, so this became our project for the duration of her training.

The training takes place on the individual's computer, which overall works best as within the institution a variety of systems are supported. Participants become familiar with how to do things on their own computer, whereas if we were to use a CSED computer, things would be set up differently. It also means that if they have things set up inappropriately for creating Web pages, Jo can either alter them or ask the lecturer to flag the problem to their IT support person. It has been known for us to come across people still using older monitors that display only 16 colours – this makes it very difficult to design good Web pages or even to use the Web. This way of working does mean Jo has to be prepared to be flexible because of the different systems and set-ups that she may come across, as well as the variety of software that people use.

The training is run at the pace of the individual and in the style that works best for him or her. Everyone has different ways of learning: some people like to go through the training step by step while Jo is there, others like to work through the booklet and use the sessions partly for trouble-shooting, some progress very quickly and others more slowly. Some need seven or eight sessions, others only one or two, but being flexible allowed us to meet people where they were. By having one-to-one training these different needs and problems could be catered for while still having the same aim of producing some Web pages to support their students.

So, overall, there are good and justifiable reasons why the training is conceived this way, and it had produced its benefits. But problems keep crowding Jo as she goes about her work. She wondered about it as she got up to go to George's session and the phone rang. It was George: 'Sorry, there's an urgent departmental meeting – I'll have to cancel,' bemoaned George. Jo realized that she really must do something. Being flexible was one thing, but her work was being compromised.

What would you do?
Do you think the benefits of this kind of training outweigh the costs?

PART 2

Jo's most significant problem was the high degree of cancellation. Cancellations have a greater effect on one-to-one training than group courses.

The reasons for cancellations are many and varied, ranging from sickness, child illness, hospital appointments, writing grant proposals, covering colleagues' teaching, subject review, assessing students and visiting students on placements, to forgetting appointments and bad planning.

Obviously these things don't happen to academic staff more than to other categories of staff. However, when you are training 12 people on a normal IT course, if one or two have to cancel then the course can still go ahead and no one blinks an eye or worries too much. But when you are dealing with people one-to-one, a couple of cancellations affect the week quite significantly.

What could we do? We considered measures such as charging for missed appointments but we felt that this would damage the good relationships that were being built and were needed for the project to work effectively. Also, many of the people who sign up for training hear about us through word of mouth, and one of the things all the participants appreciate is the flexibility we offer.

The question of whether one-to-one training is too expensive must also be addressed. It is of course true that one-to-one tuition is a more expensive use of time than traditional courses. So, there is a natural pressure towards running group-based training. However, it is important to think about which is the more effective form of training for this particular group of staff, whose profile is that they do not in general attend training courses and are hard pressed in the amount of time they have to develop Web pages.

With respect to cancellations, we decided that we wanted to remain as flexible as possible while encouraging people to keep their appointments. As a result Jo tends to fully book herself for a week on the basis that at least two people will cancel, which then gives her the time to do any necessary administration or document writing. This usually works out, and if Jo needs to do a greater degree of writing she allots more time for herself.

As to the one-to-one versus group-based training, we have tried the group approach with academics as part of this project, but it was not well supported due to other demands on their time. We had arranged for 10 academics from a particular school to attend two half-day sessions, on using the Web effectively, and an introduction to creating Web pages that would then be followed by individual tuition to help people create the pages they wanted to support students. The second of these was cancelled due to a member of staff leaving and the rest of the group having to take the strain as far as teaching commitments were concerned. In the end only the first session on how to use the Web effectively went ahead and only two people attended. It seems to be very difficult to get several academics together at any one time due to other pressures on their time. In fact it's not always that easy to arrange an appointment with just one lecturer!

A further useful element of the one-to-one training is the possibility for trouble-shooting. Some people try to take advantage of this and start asking questions about all different parts of the hardware and software when the training is specifically for Web use and Web page production. Where the questions are quick and straightforward or it is important for basic computer literacy, Jo does her best to answer them and recommends that people attend the appropriate CSED course where relevant. Nonetheless she feels it is important to focus them as much as possible, otherwise the training suffers and there is the possibility they may get confused by trying to learn too many different things at once.

Related to the above point, it is sometimes found that academic staff who book for the training have little or no basic understanding of how their computer works, which is why they take the opportunity to ask lots of general questions about their machine. Understanding file management and directory structures is an essential part of being able to create Web pages and this is something Jo has to go through. Initially she considered recommending them to go on an appropriate training course to gain the necessary skills before going through the Web training, but felt that people would probably not attend this training nor then come back for the Web training. So as file management and directory structures are so closely involved with creating a site, she has built these into the Web training to be covered if need be.

There tends to be quite a high degree of enthusiasm for the training, especially as it's one-to-one. However, as people realize creating a useful functional site is actually quite hard work it becomes more difficult to motivate them to do the work and not just go through the training. This, of course, directly relates to the fact that academics don't have enough time to dedicate to the pages and many of the people who progress do a lot of the work in their own time. There aren't really any rewards or incentives for people to take up the Web training and produce a site for their students. Those people who come on the training tend to already see the benefit either for themselves and/or their students and so have a certain degree of motivation. We have introduced some templates that people can use to minimize the amount of work and are in the process of expanding the number of these. Staff can then place their content into a pre-existing framework.

What gets identified regularly as one of the biggest problems faced by academic staff is that they do not have enough time for preparing and producing material for the Web. Developing an initial set of pages can be quite a daunting experience and beyond that the material needs to be kept up to date. We have looked at ways of overcoming this and are always rethinking the remit of the role and different ways that the problem could be attacked. Web templates can cut down the amount of work that people have to do in creating their site from scratch and there seems little sense in reinventing the wheel every time. However, it does mean that people need good general knowledge to be able to manipulate pages and fit them to their own purposes, especially as everyone wants to do things slightly differently. This only partly deals with the problem, and we still need to investigate ways of making the process easier for academic staff. The real step forward in this area will be when the university implements an automated system for publishing material either on the intranet or Internet.

Following the Web training, the help available to academic staff varies greatly from school to school. Some schools have a Web manager who can provide support, but others have Web managers in name only who don't know as much as the lecturers about creating pages. In fact in several cases the lecturer who has been through the training is probably the most knowledgeable person in the department. There have been several ways we have been starting to address this problem.

We have recently introduced a range of new modules to provide further or extended training that lecturers can take up according to need and interest. This provides people with continuity and further support. One of the new modules is Web consultancy, which enables discussion about a particular project or new course that academic staff want to put on the Web and deals with issues of design and navigation as well as layout and content of the pages. This module could be taken on an individual or small group basis.

Jo also hopes to develop a network of lecturers who have been through the Web training so they can exchange information and ideas, and discuss and investigate important issues about creating Web pages.

CASE REPORTERS' DISCUSSION

This case concerns the training and preparation of academic staff to enable them to use new technology. Staff of an academic development unit have perceived a lack of support in the application of Web technology within their university and 'filled the gap' by providing one-to-one training for lecturers keen to offer a 'Web presence' for their subjects. In doing this they have been quite successful. There has been a good response to booking up the training from academic staff, and a good deal of positive feedback about the project has been received.

However, this begs the question of the cost of such a venture and what will happen as more and more lecturers teach at least part of their subjects online. Issues such as the maintenance and updating of Web sites will become increasingly pressing, and the university will clearly need to set strategic directions and provide resources to support the growing Web presence.

Another implicit question is just how skilled should academic staff be in Web page design and development. Clearly academics have had to come to grips with a whole range of new technologies in recent decades (word-processing and e-mail being two prime examples), but is it reasonable to expect them to also become Web publishers?

So far the one-to-one approach with academic staff has worked well, particularly because of the lecturers' seeming reluctance to attend normal courses. As the university develops systems to be able to automate the process of creating Web pages and converting existing material to HTML, the content of the training will necessarily change to accommodate these developments.

CHAPTER 13

THE RELUCTANT SOFTWARE DEVELOPERS

Case reporters: Leonard Webster and David Murphy

Issues raised

The issue in this case is whether to use readily available software or to create a new software tool for an online learning environment. A key issue is the extent to which principles of good teaching and learning influence the decision.

Background

This case study concerns the first of four subjects of the Graduate Certificate in Higher Education from Monash University, a multi-campus institution based in Australia. The course is the responsibility of the Centre for Higher Education Development (CHED), which has a group of seven academics, who were involved (preparing content or designing the learning environment) in developing the semester-long subject, 'Designing for Learning'. Development began in the latter half of 1998, in preparation for the first cohort in semester one of 1999 of 40 participants, all Monash academics seeking to improve their teaching skills.

PART 1

We didn't want to create software. With eight months to go before the course commenced, work on the first subject in the Graduate Certificate began, with David coordinating the subject team. Although the curriculum was largely in place, both content and process attracted vigorous debate as the subject team grappled with their first major project. With varying discipline backgrounds and teaching experience in the group, it took some time to reach an agreed position on the basic underpinning approach to learning that would be adopted for the course. One of the guiding principles was to use an activity-based approach, where learning was active, engaging and relevant to the teaching practice of the students. The subject team agreed that an online component, in combination with face-to-face sessions and print-based learning materials, was essential to the success of the subject and ultimately the course.

The responsibility for this online development fell primarily on the authors. Both of us had previous experience in the development and design of multimedia resources for open and distance education. However, the final form this activity-based online environment might take was unclear.

Influencing our thoughts was the need for flexibility in both time and access to materials to enable busy university staff to undertake the subject. Those enrolled in the subject had teaching commitments and were employed full time in the university, resulting in restricted opportunity for face-to-face meetings during the teaching semester. Further, experienced teachers with many years of teaching in higher education would be working with those who were new or relatively new to higher education. This created an opportunity for collaboration that we were determined not to lose in utilizing an online learning environment, and was to become a key factor in the final decision.

The problem of finding an online tool that would give both access and flexibility as well as foster the activity, engagement and notions of collaborative learning embedded in the subject design and learning outcomes, nagged at us for many weeks. Members of the development team were keen, in particular, to emulate the kinds of interaction that took place in staff development workshops, where participants shared experiences and came to a shared understanding of concepts. A particular workshop activity successfully used by our colleagues provided a special challenge. For the activity, participants work in small groups, addressing questions of factors that produce good and bad learning experiences. Ideas and examples are shared, so that participants can begin to see patterns of responses emerge. How was this to be done in an online environment with something more creative and engaging than the usual electronic discussion group?

In searching for the solution a consultant was commissioned to report on a range of commercially available software tools. The report produced outlined the features of WebCT, Top Class and others, and mapped these against our needs. The outcome was anything but promising, simply confirming that we were looking for something different, beyond the standard communications, presentation of information and management features that seemed to dominate such software. The available systems with their established interactions forced a particular method of teaching that was incompatible with the underpinnings of the course. In particular, we could not see how our desired notions of collaboration could be addressed. Reluctantly, we began to realize that we might have to pursue the option of creating our own software tool.

Over a number of weeks we discussed many options only to abandon them for reasons of scope, resources or inappropriate features. We became aware of the risks that were developing as we faced the key decision of whether to stick with our vision of online learning and try to make it a reality, or take a safer route and use an established system. The need to finalize a direction for the online environment came to a climax one day in David's office as we sat around discussing the subject and how to design the online environment. As usual, we sat at the table in the middle of the office, with bits of paper covered in draft screens and maps with scribbled notes appended. We had an idea of what we were after, but couldn't see how it could be achieved.

Whatever the decision it had to be simple (given the development time frame and resources) and made quickly, as the remainder of the team had commenced developing material for the subject, preparing content and sifting through online resources. Most importantly, they needed to know what was going to be possible with the online activities, the core of the learning environment. It would become more difficult to implement any solution, indeed convince the team members of the worth of the approach, if they reached a point where considerable reworking and increased effort were required. It was with a feeling of greater pressure that we struggled towards a solution. 'I can see what we want, but just can't see how we can do it!' said David in some desperation.

What should drive the decision: modifying the teaching approach to match available software, or developing software to match the teaching approach? What are the risks involved with either decision?
Irrespective of the 'ideal' approach, what would you have done in this situation? What do you think actually happened?

PART 2

Rightly or wrongly, we were set on the risky strategy of developing a new software tool. As we sat at the table, the discussion kept returning to the face-to-face workshops, how participants share understanding, and how this is shaped and developed by collaborative learning. Driven by this need, we focused on the essential elements of what we thought we were after.

Bit by bit, a picture began to emerge. First, participants would need individual work areas to complete and store online activities. This was the equivalent of them reflecting on their own experiences or developing their own work and ideas. This work area would become the core of their learning. But the individual 'worksite' (the name suggested by Len) would need to be much more than that – it must incorporate a special feature that allowed people to select and view the responses of others to given activities. Len had been working on a related problem in another project concerning some online tutorials we were developing, and suggested a way of answering the challenge.

The basic idea was to use a database to store responses to activities that could be accessed and shared by staff and students. Essentially, we wanted participants to be able to complete activities in a personalized online environment, but at the same time be able to view the responses of others with a simple search facility. This would become the key functionality of 'InterLearn', the name eventually suggested for the software tool by David (suggesting 'interactive learning on the Internet').

Once we hit on the initial ideas, a talented programmer and a creative graphic artist who had worked on other CHED projects were brought in to help turn the vision into reality. We wanted to take the first online module of the subject, develop it into an interactive learning environment, and then use it as a template for the other four shorter modules. One of the key requirements of the early activities was the online equivalent of the face-to-face workshop activity discussed above – that is, participants were to reflect on what learning was all about, then somehow share their thoughts with others in the class. Essentially, they were to complete a series of online activities, then have a look at what others were writing in order to analyse and synthesize the collective understanding of the class.

But would it work? Against the project was the short development time, and the serious risk that it may not come together in time. Over a period of not much more than three months, the online component of the subject began to take shape, with ongoing discussions with the programmer guiding the evolving look and feel of the software. At the same time, David worked on the draft content submitted by his colleagues, maintaining the activity focus and continually striving to cut down the amount of content. It was all good stuff, but there was just too much of it!

With six weeks to go, the first fully functional version of the subject was put on the server. The following four weeks were spent checking functionality, links and the effectiveness of design features along with analysis of its robustness. This resulted in further iterations and tweaking to get a workable resource. One example was a change to the search facility, to have it open in a separate browser window. This allows a student to make comments in the relevant activity box in one window while engaging in searching and analysing other's contributions in another. All was ready – just – but would the students warm to the new learning environment? Most of the people who would take the course had never learnt or taught in an online environment before. We already knew that some were anxious about it. What should we do?

What could the team do to prepare participants who had never worked in an online learning environment before?
What do you think would be the major concerns of students?
What do you think was the reaction of students to the new environment?

PART 3

InterLearn was demonstrated at introductory workshop sessions and participants were sent a global e-mail to welcome them and encourage them to get started. Its use was also outlined in a printed study guide for the subject, and faculty-based computer support staff were alerted to possible difficulties. The development team sat back and nervously waited for responses to start appearing on the database.

Thankfully, contributions began to appear, slowly at first but growing quickly until nearly all participants were engaged with the subject materials. A student even posted on the discussion group before the first teacher's welcoming comment was made. Not only that, but the quality of the postings was refreshingly high, as the worksite began to take on a life of its own and the students became an interactive group.

After the first year of use, student responses to the online environment were very positive and encouraging. Evaluation of the use of InterLearn in the Graduate Certificate has indicated that course participants welcome the approach, and feedback by students (themselves university teachers) includes remarks such as:

> I am particularly happy with the activity system adopted in the course under different modules. The activity system allows me to build my knowledge gradually in a very flexible way. It also allows me to share others' experience and gain from their experience and knowledge. Another good reason is that I can practise what I learnt from others in my own class and add that experience to activities.
>
> Reading the various responses of other people is a great way of getting a better picture of what the class thinks as a whole.

InterLearn has now been used in all four subjects of the Graduate Certificate in Higher Education, and is beginning to be applied more widely within Monash University. However, there are aspects of its design that could be improved, and it has yet to be used in other contexts. It is a focused software tool that is not suited to all online learning environments, and would require further investment to make it commercially viable. Although the functionality of InterLearn will not be significantly extended, some minor refinements are currently being undertaken, including improvement of the search function and upgrading of the maintenance module.

One final observation of the work so far is the monitoring of workload for teachers using the InterLearn-supported activities in the Graduate Certificate subjects. It is generally agreed by the teaching staff that interactivity between students in online courses can be stimulated without adding substantially to the overall teaching load.

Did the development turn out as you expected?
Why do you think this team in particular went with the riskier option?
Are there any lessons to be taken from this case for your own course development and teaching?

CASE REPORTERS' DISCUSSION

Teachers in higher education are increasingly being faced with the challenge of offering at least part of their subjects online. Many institutions are focusing on particular software platforms or solutions that bring their own set of problems, but most academics are still faced with elements of choice in what to put online and how to structure the learning experience of their students. How much the creativity of the teacher is stifled because of the restriction of commercial systems with constrained and limited interactions is debatable.

Nevertheless, there was definitely a sense of adventure and risk-taking as we embarked on the course design and development. The main reasons that the project succeeded appear to be:

- a planned, team-based approach;
- the maintenance of a pedagogical focus – the technology served this focus, rather than driving the project;
- use of experienced staff in both teacher education and flexible learning;
- keeping the software development modest and focused on specific aims – there was never a sense of creating a new all-encompassing application;
- 'getting the mixture right' – using technologies appropriately and responding to the learners' needs and context, especially with respect to interaction/independence; and
- maintaining a vision of what the software tool was to achieve.

There was also an acceptance that many decisions would need to be made 'on the hoof'. That does not mean that decisions were made lightly, but it was recognized that problems had to be addressed swiftly, and that choices would not always be easy.

At the same time, the team were acutely aware of the credibility challenges they faced with respect to their teaching approach, appropriate use of technology, and development of a rich and justifiable teaching and learning environment. Staff developers (the teachers) in this case are wide open to (often misinformed) criticism concerning their lack of awareness of the constraints to teaching in the 'real world' and that good educational theory is all very well but is not realistic in the participants' teaching situation. Added to this is the particular need to demonstrate the use of technology for good rather than retrogressive educational purposes. A considerable amount of credibility was therefore on the line when this course opened, which may have influenced the decision to go with the more educationally justifiable decision. However, having taken that route, had the software not worked properly, or had there been major problems of any kind, the results could have been very serious for credibility in all areas.

This also relates to the issue of resourcing and the environment in which the case study took place. The Director of the Centre, who was also a member of the team, strongly encouraged innovation, displayed trust in team members and provided the resources (both time and funds) required to see the project through. The environment in which the case took place was thus conducive to experimentation and the opportunity to create a novel and collaborative learning environment.

Perhaps not obvious in the case is the use of outsourcing in the development process. A preliminary analysis to speed the review of available commercial systems at the time was outsourced to a consultant. Further, once the initial ideas were in place, a programmer and a graphic artist who had worked on other CHED projects were contracted to help turn the vision into reality.

For the development team, one exciting outcome is the conviction that there can be a deeper level of interaction using Web-based approaches. Perhaps the most important lessons are allowing the technology to be driven by the needs of students, and to be based on approaches that are activity based, relevant and engaging for the learner.

CHAPTER 14

THE GREAT COURSEWARE GAMBLE

Case reporter: Bridget Somekh

Issues raised

This case explores issues arising from the search for new technological solutions, specifically for discipline-specific courseware, to the changing needs in higher education.

Background

The case study outlines an example of a funded courseware development project that ran for three years, from 1992 to 1995 in UK universities. The project was one of 43 projects funded by the Higher Education Funding Council (HEFC) in the first round of the UK's Teaching and Learning Technology Programme (TLTP). Although it was unusually ambitious, the project faced opportunities and problems that were common to all 43 and in that sense it can be said to have been typical of early TLTP projects.

PART 1

It was a time of great jubilation. In the summer of 1992, the Head of the Accountancy Sector of the School of Information Systems at the 'lead university' heard from the HEFC that he had been awarded a TLTP grant of just over £1 million to develop computer-based courseware over a three-year period as a learning resource for non-specialist students of accountancy. Within days he received a card from the Vice-Chancellor of his university congratulating him on this achievement.

Although channelled through a single lead university, the funds were in fact awarded to a consortium of four institutions, geographically spread over a wide area of England and Scotland. A full-time research assistant (RA) was to be based in each, responsible to the Director and his three partners. This team of four RAs were responsible for software development, led by a project manager based at the lead university and appointed by the Director. Representatives of 21 other universities in England, Scotland and Wales made up the project Advisory and Associate members (A&A) group, who, with their students, constituted a client group of potential users. I was employed by the project for half my time and based, as I had been for the previous seven years, in an educational research centre at the lead university. As set out in the grant proposal, I was responsible for educational consultancy and formative evaluation, and for some elements of summative evaluation.

The project was ambitious and innovative in its design, as demonstrated first in the appointment of a multidisciplinary team. The four consortium partners were all senior academics in university departments of Accountancy, but the four RAs were appointed to bring specialisms to the team: an electronic designer, an educationalist with a background in a business school, an accountant and a computer programmer. In addition, the evaluator (myself) had previously led projects developing the effective use of ICT in schools and university departments of education.

The project team were appointed with little delay and began work with enthusiasm. It was recognized that project management would be complex with collaborating partners located at such a distance from each other, so a programme of regular meetings was set up. Between meetings electronic communications would be used, both for e-mail and file transfer. The team meetings were residential affairs with opportunities for 'bonding experiences' including go-karting on one occasion and always time after dinner spent in the bar. Meetings rotated around the four participating universities but accommodation was provided in hotels rather than university residences, indicating perhaps a touch of the culture of the Business Schools in which some of the Accountancy departments were located.

Although TLTP funding was for development work, not research, it was of considerable importance for all the participants to use this opportunity to further their research since their future academic careers would depend upon it. Some members of the consortium, as well as the project manager, were also very interested in the possibility of commercial development of the product after the end of the funded period. The intention was, therefore, to fulfil the aims of the TLTP contract but to carry out research and innovative development work as an integral part of the process of producing the courseware. Whereas the TLTP sponsors wanted courseware to be developed using existing software tools, such as QuestionTime and Authorware, the decision was taken to use a new software 'tool library' (then about to come on the market) for the main phase of the work, with a programming language to fill the gaps where this proved insufficient. Meanwhile, the first year's work would focus on the production of a prototype using Authorware.

The aim was to begin with an exploratory process to establish the design of the product, including both its contents and its user interface, before moving on to the more time-consuming and painstaking work of producing the permanent product. The development platform would be the Apple Macintosh because of its then superior design facilities and related software packages, but the delivery platform would be both the Apple Mac and the PC, since the latter was the main installed hardware base in university departments of Accountancy at the time. The concept was of delivery of the software on portable machines which students could use any place, any time (one publicity photo for the local paper showed a team member using a portable PC in the bath).

These and other software/hardware decisions were contentious, involving lengthy discussions between the Director, the three other consortium partners and the project manager. As evaluator, my role was to listen, note all the key points put forward in defence of each viewpoint, and give advice when asked. Inevitably, I became involved in the internal 'politics' of the project as a result of my self-appointed role to assist the team in building common values and purposes.

At their first three-day project meeting, the project manager and the RAs decided to design the courseware around a 'metaphor'. This would have multiple functions: as a unifying thematic concept underpinning the content, a flexible framework for the programming, and a user interface and aid to navigating in a hypertext environment. The metaphor would have the characteristics of a 'microworld', providing the user with a range of choices while exploring a virtual environment. Learning and exploration were intended to be integral with one another and the environment should have the feel of a computer game. It should be both compelling and fun.

The prototype provided two metaphors: an exploration of an accountant's office, or an exploration of a shopping arcade. In the first of these the 'user-learner' visited different rooms and desks in the office and was offered tasks involving the acquisition and use of accountancy knowledge appropriate to the person who worked at that desk – the learner was in the role of an interloper exploring the office illicitly. In the second metaphor the 'user-learner' opened a Pandora's Box trunk allowing four 'monsters' to escape into a shopping arcade, and was then given the task of finding them and 'capturing' them by visiting different businesses and shops in the arcade and solving accountancy problems appropriate to the people who worked there.

The prototype was presented to the consortium partners and the A&A group, and out of this process emerged the decision to develop the main product using the shopping arcade metaphor. A factor in the decision was the greater enthusiasm of the development team for this second metaphor, for three possible reasons. First, the shopping arcade environment gave greater scope for developing 'relevant' accountancy tasks for the learner; second, it gave much more scope for imaginative design; and third, with its four funky monsters it had much more of the 'feel' of a computer game.

In addition to learning accountancy by playing the game contained in the shopping arcade, information about accountancy was available to learners through a searchable lexicon. Very large quantities of text could, in fact, be accessed either directly through the lexicon or indirectly through seeking further assistance while investigating the problems in the shopping arcade. A map of the navigation structure of the package could also be accessed so that the students could identify which bits of content they had covered and where they had got to in going through the total courseware. Finally, there were self-test questions relating to each section of the content. The learner was free to choose which part of the software to access and could move easily from one part to another – for example, from the shopping arcade to the searchable lexicon.

The central purpose of the project was to serve the needs of the student learner, and the team explored a wide range of learning theories with the aim of ensuring that the software would address learners' needs. In addition, in my role as educational consultant and evaluator, I was asked to provide the development team with advice on learning theories to inform the design process. As a result, the courseware that was developed attempted to take account of, for example, the computer's ability to 'situate' learning in realistic (although virtual) contexts, the stimulus and recall effects that are embedded in games software, the importance of motivation for learning and the impor- tance of immediate feedback for learning.

We were fired up and we were ready. All was in place for the fulfilment of the project's ambitious aims. Or was it?

What possible problems and issues do you imagine might arise as the project unfolded?
What do you think was the outcome?

PART 2

The project started with enthusiasm and its purpose related to real needs in higher education. But significant problems and deficiencies began to appear. For example, the issue of getting the courseware into use was seen by the sponsor, HEFC, as merely a matter of overcoming the 'not invented here syndrome' – hence, every project had to consist of a consortium of partners and each consortium had to work with a large number of other universities. In attempting to give ownership to all, resources became fragmented without any real pay-off.

The consortia approach, required by HEFC, resulted in this and all other TLTP projects attempting to work in close collaboration over large distances.

Collaboration is always difficult, but between individuals located at a distance from one another it becomes extremely problematic, maybe impossible. Electronic communications appeared at first to be an answer, but the infrastructure was not properly in place and one of the universities was not linked to the others electronically. The cabling was promised... and did not come... and did not come. It left the RA based at this university, who was responsible for developing the content, to work very much alone. This was probably a major reason why the text/content parts of the final product never appeared to be properly integrated with the pursuit of the monsters in the shopping arcade. Moving from the arcade to the 'content' entailed moving out of the rich, colourful environment of the microworld into a text-based electronic workbook.

Further, the way that the project was structured, with its far-flung consortium, the necessity of spending considerable funding on travel and residential meetings, the problems of – and later lack of any effective – coordination and support, and the pressure on individuals brought about by uncertainties of employment and the need to deliver in a fiercely difficult new field, led to serious deterioration of morale. The team became fractured. One member became terminally ill. Another got divorced. The RAs divided into two singles and one working pair, separated from each other by serious disagreements between the consortium partners to whom they each, severally, owed allegiances. Sometimes there was secrecy over the spending of funds, so that the project secretary was required to keep overseas trips secret from other consortium members.

And my role? Far from helping the team to develop common values and purposes, I became an object of the Director's suspicion. As I visited each team I became more and more the recipient of confidences about problems, and took more and more the role of representing and explaining the views of one partner to the others. The Director's instinct was for strong management and mine was for democratic decision making. These were conflicting values. No agreement could be reached on principles of procedure setting out ethical guidelines for the conduct of the evaluation or its reporting. Without permission even to speak about the evaluation methods, it was inevitable that at some point it would be thought that I had transgressed. As a result, the evaluator and the team parted company and a new evaluator (one of my colleagues), who had much less understanding of the project's purposes, was appointed. The team were left with incomplete advice from the first evaluator, so that when the final evaluation report was published by my successor (without the agreement of the Director) it took issue with features of the courseware that some team members felt had been developed in response to guidance from the first evaluator.

So, after three years, the outcomes were disappointing:

- the software was never finalized in a wholly debugged form because time and money ran out;

- user reactions from academic accountants were confused and broadly negative;
- user reactions from a small sample of school leavers were initially positive, but were not sustained in the light of probing questions from my successor as evaluator;
- the software is not used in the teaching of accountancy (although much other TLTP software is used to varying extents in a range of academic departments); and
- the proposed commercialization of the project never materialized.

The unfinished state of the courseware made it impossible to give it proper trials with students, but through demonstrating it to several cohorts of Master's students in subsequent years, I have elicited a range of opinions about it, including:

- the shopping arcade is an exceptionally attractive and imaginative interface;
- the monsters are childish and silly (a few students under the age of 25, however, really like them – response to the monsters may be related to age);
- the text/content is just chunks of textbook on the screen and is not integrated with the game;
- the moves from the shopping arcade interface to the Windows interface on the Mac or PC are jarring and non-intuitive;
- the links between the monsters and the accountancy problems that have to be 'solved' are very artificial or non-existent;
- the choice between different ways of accessing the content is confusing rather than empowering; and
- the self-tests are good, but no better than they would be in textbooks.

CASE REPORTER'S DISCUSSION

Why did this great courseware gamble not pay off? There are many possible answers to this question and no certainties. First it is clear that the project was overambitious. This originated at the stage of bidding for the funding. Of the 43 projects funded in the first round, this project was awarded the most money – approximately one eighth of the entire budget. This placed an enormous pressure on the consortium members. Arguably, the members of the committee who awarded the funding had unrealistic expectations of what could be achieved by academics (amateurs?) in a three-year period. Certainly, those writing the proposals felt impelled to offer a great deal to secure the funding. What they offered was mainly quantified in terms of student time-on-machine using the proposed courseware – what was later called by a member of the committee, 'BSH' (bums, seats, hours). This was undoubtedly what the committee wanted. Another expectation was that the products would be capable of commercial exploitation, although this was problematic from the start because the initial products, having been paid for by public money, had to be made available free to all UK universities. The only viable market was therefore overseas and this was unlikely to be appropriate for courseware developed explicitly to teach British methods of accountancy.

Then there was the confusion in the purposes of higher education itself. This was one of the first major funding initiatives designed to support teaching rather than research, but the project personnel could not afford to neglect the demands on them to publish research papers. This was especially true because the contracts of the project manager and the RAs were issued for one year only, and renewed only after the sponsors had approved the previous year's work. Therefore, in the summer of each year, five key members of the project team became seriously unsettled, unsure if their jobs would continue in the autumn. The project manager became inactive, team meetings ceased and individuals were left alone as major deadlines approached. The consortium partners and the project manager produced conference papers with a view to publication, but the four RAs did not, perhaps because the rules of the academic game were not sufficiently clear to them, or because their subservient role to the consortium partners acted as a constraint upon them.

The user base in the universities was also too immature for such an ambitious project. Courseware of this kind needed to make use of multimedia facilities and at the very least the state-of-the art machines of 1992. And academic staff were unreceptive to using the courseware when it began to be ready for trials. Had it ever been finished – even if it had lived up to its original underpinning vision – it would probably have been too innovative to win over accountancy lecturers of the time to use it.

The development platform was also too immature. In the first year, the prototyping approach presented problems because Authorware was too inflexible, leading to more time than expected having to be spent developing special features using other programming techniques. In the main phase, the problems of 'writing down' to the level of the Windows 480 platform were depressing and time-consuming, the software 'tool library' did not emerge from the commercial producer when promised and portability between Macs and PCs was not as seamless as had been expected.

This analysis should, of course, be set in the context of the 'mad scramble' to use ICT to reduce the costs of teaching, which is misguided and almost certainly unattainable. Although this case occurred nearly 10 years ago, all the issues it raises are obvious in the current scramble to put courses on the Web. The things that went wrong were almost inevitable given the situation in which the team found itself.

If we want higher education to make effective use of new technologies we need a much more integrated approach. Focusing on the delivery of content through discipline-specific courseware is insufficient. There needs to be a whole-institution development plan, along the lines suggested by Laurillard (1993). Courses need to be redesigned with more varied teaching patterns, including interactive computer-supported group discussions as well as student self-study. Departmental structures also probably need to be redesigned to include interdisciplinary teams rather than academic cultural cabals.

REFERENCE

Laurillard, D (1993) *Rethinking University Teaching: A framework for the effective use of educational technology*, Routledge, London

CHAPTER 15

POETIC SEEING

Case reporters: Lee Kar Tin and Wong Lai Fong

Issues raised

The issue raised in this case is the implementation of a curriculum reform policy without the necessary enabling conditions to carry this through in the schools.

Background

In 1998 the Hong Kong Government announced a wide-ranging set of information technology (IT) policies for schools, which included the challenge to art teachers to enhance traditional art lessons with the use of IT. Most teachers in Hong Kong schools were not trained in IT and so were unable to respond to the challenge. As a teacher educator at the Hong Kong Institute of Education (HKIEd), Oi Vong faced the task of helping her students (schoolteachers) develop competence and confidence in relevant skills and the capacity to use these skills in schools where established teachers were unlikely to be able to offer support.

PART 1

Oi Vong was excited at the prospect of helping her students make effective use of IT. The Curriculum Development Council had identified the unique contribution of a balanced art education to the development of students' creativity, imagination and aesthetic perception. It wanted to encourage good use of cross-curricular links to promote the use of artistic senses, such as musical activities for the learning of languages and drama for simulating life experiences.

Oi Vong was keen to be part of the process of change and felt that her students needed to better understand their own pedagogical practices if they were to deal with the problems they would meet in schools, and make effective use of new and emerging IT possibilities. She was convinced that the effective use of IT in primary art meant that all teachers had to rethink their teaching strategies in order to accommodate the new approaches. Teachers of art, not just student teachers, had to be ready to engage in the pedagogical shifts that were needed.

Believing that art education in the schools was not successfully implementing the government's broad, cross-curricula aims, Oi Vong decided to attempt to do so through the use of multimedia. She believed that traditional methods of art teaching, which applied static, linear and disparate design models, did not lend themselves to multimedia development. She therefore faced not just a teacher education project, but one that involved rebuilding the art education curriculum from first principles.

In the past, visuals had been used in Hong Kong schools as writing stimuli to help improve students' appreciation of visual elements by perceiving and drawing pictures from poetry, musical sounds and songs. Oi Vong saw this as a starting point for thinking about ways in which multimedia materials could be used in art teaching. She saw the need to:

- explore the linguistic images and structures that support multi-sensory educational materials;
- review the use of computers in conducting applied research in art, music and poetry education;
- examine how technology can afford the greatest effects on the development of the artistic sensitivity, cognition and emotion of a student; and,
- encourage development of primary and secondary school students' appreciation, understanding and knowledge of the visual arts in a cross-disciplinary approach.

In using multimedia to deliver video, images and text to the classroom, Oi Vong hoped to create a learning environment that would enable student teachers to use multimedia and computers as educational resources. As an integrated and interactive system, this would be important for the future development of arts education in kindergarten, primary and secondary schools as well as in teacher education.

Oi Vong's key interest was the use of language underlying visual phenomena, the main question in her mind being: 'How can teachers more effectively help students to develop their own visual literacy?' The new policy had provided an opportunity for her, but she had a number of problems and issues to consider.

What problems do you see ahead for Oi Vong?

Where do you think she should begin?
How can she get student teachers, schools and others to share her vision?

PART 2

As a lecturer, artist and poet, Oi Vong was particularly interested in the unique attributes of multimedia as a delivery system. She believed that multimedia could be used to address the needs of visual art, music and literature teaching. She wanted to transform the audio-visual field from a static notion of 'educational technology' into something much more creative. She named her project, 'Making Sense of Poetic Seeing: Computerized Capabilities in Visualizing the Verbal'.

She began with what she knew best. At the start of the project, in February 1999, she wrote 20 poems to represent the initial resources for purposes of responding, representing and visualizing. From these poems, students in a selected primary school, without being given any guiding styles to adhere to, produced a series of experimental paintings covering a variety of topic areas. These materials were then used as instructional samples for further development.

The emphasis throughout the project was on introducing children to visual elements and the learning of design principles. The poems were used to demonstrate the elements particular to visual arts such as colour, texture, shapes and features common to all art forms such as rhythm, unity, conflict, tone and mood. Each artistic element had an associated vocabulary. Students could learn the language through planned interactions with pictures, music and sounds, and by reading and reciting poems. The students utilized two types of imaginative processes: starting with the text and arriving at the visual image, and starting with a visual image and arriving at verbal expression. Both methods produced associations, connotations, metaphors and symbols that cannot be found in either pictures or poems alone. These materials therefore maximized the potential of the 'verbal energy of poetry' and 'visual richness and diversity' of painting. And multimedia made it all possible as changes were captured on computer screen and could be played back to the students.

The project was a cooperative effort, which required the student teachers to develop new competencies and foundation skills. These competencies and skills were based on processes that included the following:

- Using multimedia tools: use of the computer to create, organize and maintain instructional portfolios (students had to learn how to scan 'live' images, download images from the Web and CD ROM, and become proficient in the use of Photoshop and Authorware on the PC).
- Basic skill in art and design: exploring the visual factors that contribute to successful computer multimedia design.

- Interpersonal skill: working in teams to complete a well-designed set of presentations; interpret and communicate ideas.
- Linking skills to aesthetic and artistic problems: visualizing and thinking creatively.

Oi Vong had a vision, and had taken the first steps towards making her vision a reality.

What problems do you anticipate Oi Vong will face in moving ahead?
How can you see technology being employed in the project?

PART 3

As Oi Vong began to move more deeply into the first phase of the project, a number of problems began to arise, both technical and operational. She had previously participated in a number of workshops and a diploma course in multimedia design and development, and had applied her new skills to her teaching. With these, admittedly limited, IT skills she began to experiment with Authorware, adopting a 'learning by doing' approach. She eventually created a multimedia application that gave her the opportunity to work with other colleagues and 60 art students who had no computer background.

In order to get started, she sent her students to an introductory six-hour training session in Authorware. Despite this preparation, the first stage of implementation was difficult due to the lack of expertise, which seemed to limit the students' imagination. Further, due to a lack of funds, technical support was discontinued. Undeterred, Oi Vong saw this as a chance for continual self-improvement. She divided the project into component parts and assigned tasks to six working groups who continued to collect samples of artwork. She then spent a great deal of time collating and editing the collected samples.

Other difficulties that Oi Vong encountered included:

- the need for ongoing evaluation of the present attitudes and skill levels of student teachers;
- the gathering of all possible resources from students at all levels;
- providing classroom application for different levels; and
- evaluation of the effectiveness and outcomes of the use of different media.

Faced with these ongoing problems, Oi Vong trained her students in computer-based pedagogy related to different educational packages and implemented a 'bottom-up' rather than a 'top-down' pedagogical style that developed students' feelings and concepts from examples and applications.

She intended to let the student teachers encounter various levels of observation, analysis, interpretation and judgement on issues taken from their own
work or from other students' work. A learning environment was created for
the students in which they had to respond to a series of pedagogical questions, and formulate and reconstruct the materials they produced. It was
expected that the processes would also further develop their art vocabulary
and aesthetic sense and evoke discussion about the exemplars displayed.

Subsequently, through the cooperation of teams of student teachers at the
HKIEd, a larger range of content was collated. This included 2-D drawings,
paintings and 3-D sculptures produced by both the primary school students
and the HKIEd pre-service and in-service teachers. These materials and
resources were later used by students in other primary schools as resources for
art teaching and published on CD ROMs and in a book. The evaluation of
the project was revealing.

How would you go about evaluating this project?
How successful do you think the project turned out to be?

PART 4

Several methods of evaluation were used for both groups (student teachers
and primary school students), including observation and peer description.
The activities were judged to be worthwhile and effective, with observations
revealing that students became very involved and willingly provided feedback
and response during classroom discussion. Further, students took responsibility for their own learning, and demonstrated increased efforts to explore
ideas and produce creative materials. Both groups were able to self-evaluate
their work and engage in collaborative learning activities.

In addition, good quality was achieved in overall presentation. The
evidence included:

- emerging richness of images and literacy;
- the revealing of individual differences;
- the experience of personal power and style; and
- the expansion of meaning and feelings for the text.

Oi Vong expected that through participation students would develop very
different styles of visualization. Some factors were also expected to account
for the variations in personal learning styles (active or passive) and differences
in representation styles (expressive or constructive).

These expectations generally held true. However, during the course of the
project several questions arose which stimulated further investigation,
including: how did students with differing learning styles interact with

instructional technology and, how did students draw imagery, ideas and visual thinking in response to different multimedia material?

Although the learners were able to generate ideas from the images of the poems, they could not always generate their art products, and this was especially true for the adult students.

The project gave students time to concentrate on content representation, and avoided unnecessary frustration caused by a lack of programming or artistic skills. The approach provided students with opportunities for learning through their own perspective and insight. As part of the ongoing activity and discussions, the interactive process could also encourage both teachers and students to explore and recreate knowledge by engaging them in reworking drafts and prototypes. Students were offered the chance to develop their ideas from the poems in multiple perspectives in order to meet higher-level challenges. They commented that this approach refreshed their learning and improved their technique. They tended to experience in-depth thinking and feeling with support from the interactive learning environment.

As a result of her successes, Oi Vong's project has since been integrated into Art Studio modules offered at HKIEd for those students studying to become art teachers. The two CD ROMs contain resources to support an integration of visual arts, Chinese language literature and the music curriculum. By putting poetic texts on the soundtrack and on the screen, participants in the project are able to focus on exploring relationships between visual-verbal and audio-verbal images. The accompanying book contains primary materials of printed text and images.

CASE REPORTERS' DISCUSSION

According to Cennamo (1993), learning attitudes, the ability of a medium to present actual models demonstrating a desired behaviour, and learners' personal preferences, all contribute to ease of learning from a medium. This means that simply incorporating multimedia into an educational presentation does not necessarily help students to master a subject more easily.

By making the materials relevant to students' natural tendency and providing a structure that enhances intrinsic motivation, it was hoped that the adult participants would cultivate the potential to be teachers who could be leaders in implementing new technologies in art classrooms. An effective teacher should provide new material for a context, and create a new context for learning. To accomplish this, students must be able to increase their awareness of the culture of the tools which information technology offers.

Oi Vong's experience has shown that works of art can be used in the classroom in a way that is not narrowly focused on knowledge of the artwork for its own sake, nor solely in terms of the way it might inform children's own work, though these are important dimensions. It suggests that in developing children's visual literacy, their powers of thought and reason are challenged, and abilities in thinking can potentially be developed in ways that could be transferable to other areas of knowledge and enquiry.

The process of interrogating the art works from a variety of perspectives certainly has potential for developing children's powers of reasoning and to provide a focus for 'thinking philosophically', as can be seen from the students' ability to transform poems into artwork and vice versa.

Overall, the case provides evidence of the power of educational technology to meet the demands of curriculum reform, in this example as provided by IT policies and the aims of the Curriculum Development Council. It is all the more instructive when the case addresses particularly challenging areas of the curriculum such as creativity, imagination and aesthetic perception.

Reference

Cennamo, K S (1993) *Preconceptions of Mediated Instruction for Various Domains of Learning Outcomes,* IR 016 313

POLICY ISSUES

CHAPTER 16

WHO IS LEADING WHOM?

Case reporter: Michelle Selinger

Issues raised

This case addresses the dilemma faced by teacher educators of providing a student-led approach to developing skills in information and communication technology (ICT), while at the same time meeting statutory government requirements.

Background

This case takes place in the Institute of Education, University of Warwick, UK. The setting is teacher training and the teachers involved are university tutors and school mentors who support the practical aspect of students' preparation for teaching. Students are enrolled either for a one-year Postgraduate Certificate of Education for primary or secondary teaching or a four-year BA (QTS) course for primary only. The case reporter is an experienced academic teaching such a programme, along with a team of colleagues.

In England, all student teachers have to meet a set of standards in classroom planning, teaching and management, assessment, recording and reporting, subject knowledge, and the wider professional role of the teacher (DfEE, 1998). ICT was recently added to go alongside government plans to develop an ICT infrastructure: the 'National Grid for Learning' (DfEE, 1997). It is now a statutory requirement, therefore, that all beginning teachers in England are 'confident and competent' users of ICT in order to gain qualified teacher status.

In order to provide students with an appropriate experience to meet the ICT standards, a multimedia centre was set up to promote confidence and proficiency in the use of ICT. The Centre for New Technologies Research in

Education (CeNTRE) houses two labs and a drop-in centre equipped with networked PCs similar to those found in many newly equipped schools.

PART 1

Student teachers spend a significant proportion of their time in schools, which vary greatly in their use of ICT and the priority they give to the provision of resources. Helping students to achieve the required standards is thus difficult as schools are still, on the whole, not equipped to provide students with the experiences they need. There are many factors that contribute to this gap between the requirement and provision, including equipment, school ethos, access, time, intentions and purposes for using ICT. Student teachers encounter a whole range of ICT infrastructures when on school placements and an even greater variety of practice. Nonetheless, all beginning teachers are required by the Department for Education and Employment to know when and when not, and how to use ICT in subject teaching, and to have personal ICT capability. They are expected to be given opportunities to practise the required methods and skills in classrooms and to demonstrate their personal competence in professional contexts. Teacher education programmes find themselves having to manage the consequent gap between requirements, support and provision.

How were we to 'fill the gap'? How could we develop a programme that addressed the complex range of needs and demands? At first we tried conventional approaches, and seemingly made a good, positive start. Meetings were arranged with staff and staff development sessions set up, which resulted in variable attendance. School mentor briefings are held regularly, as it is the university's responsibility to ensure that teachers in partner schools are aware of the demands of the standards for beginning teachers to achieve qualified teacher status. These meetings alert mentors (ie teachers who are to support students on schools placements) to the standards and suggest ways in which they can help students achieve them. The briefings included an ICT slot, and paperwork explaining the situation was developed. There appeared to be a willingness to take part: many could see the potential benefits even if they were still unaware of the implications of the new statutory requirements. Ideas were put forward and some staff's eyes lit up as they talked about how they could make greater use of ICT. Two data projectors were purchased, and laptops assigned to staff to encourage them to use them in their teaching, and staff were asked to demonstrate where they planned to use ICT in their courses. The services of the ICT staff and the multimedia centre manager were offered and skills sessions were put in place for all students. We were up and running.

Our satisfaction was short-lived. Subsequent implementation was slow. There appeared to be no real realization of the statutory nature of the implementation and, where ICT was being used, it continued but without recourse to the whole ICT experience of the students. Schools were still unsure of their role in the process and, in many cases, the ICT infrastructure in the school made it difficult for many students to gain any ICT experience in a real teaching context. It seemed that we were training student teachers, knowing that they would not be able to practise what they had learnt in the schools. However, we knew that government funding had been allocated for supporting the purchase of ICT equipment and that ultimately schools would be in a better position to provide students with the experiences that would give them the necessary skills.

The situation called for a radical rethink. We decided to change tack and to adopt a different strategy to make the developments student-led. Our logic was that if staff in the university and in the schools were not able to respond fast enough, then we could increase students' awareness of the potential in the hope that this would, in turn, encourage greater staff engagement. We had to make it clear to the students that it would not always be possible to use new skills and ideas about integrating ICT in their teaching, but that by the time they finished the course, more schools would be up and running with a new infrastructure and teachers would have received training. Their skills, developed at Warwick, would be sought after and make the students extremely employable in the job market for primary teachers.

An ICT programme was developed for students and 'just-in-time' support was made available in a newly established multimedia centre that modelled a school computer network. As a result of these initiatives, we believed, student's ICT skills would be developed. The students would force the pace in the use of ICT in schools causing tutors to come forward to find out more.

How do you think this will work in practice?
What issues would you expect to emerge?

PART 2

In the early stages, we tried to find ways in which to enthuse students with ICT. We told them that they will be the teachers of the future and that schools will look to them to develop the use of ICT with pupils both in their school experience placements and in their future careers. Many rose to the challenge. One student became so excited that she wrote a proposal for her son's school for a Millennium grant. She wanted to build a butterfly garden in the school grounds and after her ICT sessions at the university she came to discuss how she might tie in a Web site to her proposal. We mapped out a Web site with Webcam facilities, links to other Web sites that had details about the types of butterflies she wanted to attract, links to ecological sites and also to school Web pages devoted to the progress of the garden as it was developed and how it looked at different times of the year, plus children's writing and art work about the garden. She saw immediately how ICT enhanced her proposal and how it might support and develop children's understanding of key concepts. Unfortunately she was unsuccessful in her bid, but this did not dampen her enthusiasm and it certainly gave her science tutors food for thought. It led them to think about other ways they might incorporate ICT into a course that already made extensive use of scientific applications of ICT with data loggers, graph plotters and spreadsheets.

Our ICT course is a single 60-hour course. We start the course with a treasure hunt, which encourages students to develop their skills in word-processing, spreadsheets, manipulating images, the Internet, logo and e-mail. We encourage students to form groups to make use of peer expertise, and staff are on hand to offer advice. For the most part students are able, with the minimum of support, to engage fully with both the problems and with the technology. At each stage they are asked to consider the elements of ICT with which they are working, and how a similar activity could be used with children, and to what purpose. Many good suggestions and questions are raised at the end of each session in feedback and discussion. We also introduce students to FirstClass as their main source of e-mail and for computer conferencing, and to this end we embed FirstClass into the treasure hunt (the clues are held there). Later in the course the students use FirstClass to post evaluations of educational software and resources they have developed with a view to accessing them from school on their next or subsequent teaching placements.

There were occasions when ad hoc direct teaching took place. A brief look at a spreadsheet was needed with one group. Another benefited from a demonstration of saving picture files from a Web page. There were also times when individuals asked for, and were given, specific help. The self-help groupings seemed to be valued, as were suggestions that whenever they felt in need of help they should ask the person next to them first. For the tutors, it was possible to stand back, listen and observe a great deal of peer support and experimentation taking place. We hope we modelled ways of working in the classroom that the students would draw on in school placements.

As well as developing a teaching programme we saw the need to develop policy across the courses. We set up a committee, which included representatives of all subjects taught in the undergraduate course. We outlined the course and asked them to tell us where it overlapped, if at all, with their ICT plans. We asked for a document from each department that outlined where they would use ICT. Where there were duplications we offered support in any way we could and also offered to alter our courses to accommodate their plans. However, some overlaps remained, but less in the second year than in the first.

We offered the services of the Multimedia Centre manager to staff. The centre was established to support staff and students and aims to provide an

ICT environment that is friendly and inviting. There is no technician and the centre manager is a 'technically minded' teacher who spent several years as an ICT coordinator in a primary school. She has encouraged staff to perceive her as support and not to ask her to do ICT-related tasks for them, such as scanning in pictures, but ask her to show them *how* to use the scanner.

We have equipped two labs with similar machines to those found in over half the schools in the UK, with the software that most schools are purchasing loaded on to the system. We keep in touch with local education authorities' ICT support staff and find out what local schools are using and what infrastructures they are developing. We can then inform our students and ensure we have the same software available so that they can try it out and develop or review support materials before going into schools to use it.

When students return from school placements we discuss their ICT experiences with them. Provision in the schools varies from one or two old BBC machines, relics from the 1980s, to fully equipped computer suites housing brand new PCs. The latter is a rarity; most schools fall somewhere between the two extremes with computer purchasing plans in train to replace Acorn computers with PCs. They do not complain that we are preparing them for experiences they have yet to meet; they seem to understand the relevance of what we do, and we do provide two sessions in the old Acorn room so they can familiarize themselves with that technology and the related software.

Students are asked to produce a portfolio of evidence that demonstrates they have met all the standards required of them within the ICT strand. We present this as the three Ps – personal, professional and pedagogical skills. The portfolio requirements include evidence of basic ICT skills that is achieved through the use of four self-study packs each with a number of small tasks that are set within a professional context. We ask students to develop a set of three differentiated worksheets for a class they have taught or are about to teach using the features of a word-processor and/or a desktop publisher, graphics packages, etc. We also ask them to indicate where and when they have used ICT in lessons in schools and to evaluate the success or otherwise of a small number of lessons, considering the extent to which they used ICT, justifying this use, and why it may have been more beneficial than using other teaching resources.

The 'just-in-time' support from the centre manager is a key feature of this whole programme. Students need to know that if they need help, it is immediately available. This seems to be an unusual feature in teacher education and resources for such posts are difficult to find. Yet students' confidence can be undermined if they are working on a task, browsing a CD ROM or surfing the Web and reach an impasse. If help is at hand, then their confidence is retained and they will be more willing to try something new. With a teaching background, the centre manager also gives advice on using ICT in schools and challenges students about the suitability or appropriateness of the tasks they are developing for using ICT in the classroom.

By offering advice and support on a daily basis we have reached a stage where every machine is fully utilized during the hours of 9 and 5, Monday to Friday. We see staff mingled in with students and by putting Drop-in Centre machines in dining areas, we have encouraged peer collaboration and support. Students are demanding more ICT and staff in the Institute are responding. Schools are relying on our students and are learning from them.

CASE REPORTER'S DISCUSSION

After a somewhat shaky start, we believe that we have developed a programme that is able to meet the needs of students while at the same time satisfying government statutory requirements. This has been achieved by addressing a number of key challenges.

First, we criticize students for not differentiating between pupils in schools, yet we are guilty of it ourselves. Not only do students come to us with varying skills and different views of the role of ICT in learning, but staff are also at varying levels. We are fortunate in that a number of staff have excellent skills; they make use of ICT regularly both in teaching main subject studies as well as in curriculum sessions. However, we need to look at a coherent model for ICT development across the whole partnership and programme. We have asked for and at last received a curriculum mapping document for ICT in the core subjects of mathematics, science and English, and for the specialist curriculum subjects so that we can produce a coherent programme for the students in which they see ICT integrated and related to curriculum targets, and so they perceive a need for professional uses of ICT and for their own personal development and productivity.

We have also realized the value of just-in-time support for both staff and students. The use of a centre manager who is *not* regarded as a technician has been crucial to this development. We offer schools an affiliation programme that enables them to send teachers in to use the facilities, and we continue to inform schools about developments in ICT at the institute through the part-nership newsletter and through access to the students' work on ICT within FirstClass. We run courses for classroom assistants who perhaps have more time to develop ICT skills, which they can use with children in the classroom, and who can perhaps suggest to teachers ways in which ICT can support some other students in their care.

In addition, we have confirmed that it is not sufficient simply to train teachers to be competent with specific software or hardware. Their skills development must be more generic, so that they become confident and competent users of ICT in the classroom. They are willing to take risks with ICT and are not concerned about changes in the platforms they encounter (Haigh, 1999).

As the reality of the statutory requirements becomes clearer, and students' conversations about the computer facilities raise staff awareness of their presence, we are receiving more requests to use the facilities or for us to team-teach with those staff who are less confident. The intention is that eventually we do not run a separate ICT course, but offer a range of workshops based on current demands, or team-teach with curriculum specialists. Our job will become one of support and development; keeping an eye out for new ways of using ICT and bringing it to the attention of schools, students and tutors alike. The partnership between schools and the Institute of Education can be strengthened both by professional links and by sharing of practice, and by using student teachers as the agents of change. The job is not over yet!

References

DfEE (1997) *Connecting the Learning Society, National Grid for Learning, The Government's Consultation Paper,* Department for Education and Employment, London

DfEE (1998) *Teaching: High status, high standards,* Department for Education and Employment, London

Haigh, G (1999) 'Building up class confidence', *TES Online,* 14 May, p 42

CHAPTER 17

TRAVELLING WITHOUT MAPS

Case reporters: Alison Littler and Jan Mahyuddin

Issues raised

This case concerns the dilemmas faced by editorial staff producing a university's distance education programme and being required to incorporate new digital technologies rapidly and 'on the hoof'. Specific issues include the need for staff development in coming to terms with online technologies, and for direction in applying them.

Background

The group of editors in this case study worked at Deakin University, a multi-campus dual-mode university in Australia. In the early 1990s Deakin, which had been developing and delivering large-scale distance courses for more than 20 years, was drawn into successive amalgamations with a number of other tertiary institutions. The most recent and largest of these institutions had no history of involvement in distance education and had developed a proliferation of courses enrolling small numbers of students. All faculties across the university were subsequently instructed to rationalize their course offerings. Immediately, this dramatically increased the volume of materials to be produced with no commensurate increase in production staff.

Late in 1996, at a public gathering, the Vice-Chancellor announced that the university would fast-track the implementation of online technologies, and that within a year all course materials would be offered online. This was a surprising announcement given that structures and processes were not yet in place to support this strategy. No central funding had been allocated for mainstreaming the production of such a volume of course materials, no 'official' involvement of editors or designers was planned, no training had been provided, and there was limited knowledge of student access to online facilities.

PART 1

'We're all struggling with a lack of guidelines for using online technologies,' Alison said to Jan and Susan as they ruminated about their work, 'so why don't we meet specifically to share what we're learning. Rosemary and Alice might like to join us too.' It was late 1997, and there was still an absence of planning and preparation for using online technologies.

Alison, as senior editor for the Arts Faculty, was constantly having to answer questions from faculty about the use of online and multimedia technologies. She was also responsible for ensuring that editors working in the Arts Faculty programme were supported when undertaking new tasks. Alison had been concerned at the lack of forward planning in anticipating change, as well as the practice of leaving editors and production staff 'out of the loop'. The general thinking about the role of editors seemed to be driven by burgeoning digital-world 'hype' that claimed anyone could develop, design and write their own materials: all that was needed was a keyboard, a spellchecker and a server.

Susan was working on a complex unit to be delivered via a Web site, using text, still images, video and audio, and including a print component, all involving difficult copyright issues. But there were no guidelines about costs, time available to be spent, funds for copyright applications, staff resources available to draw upon when required (such as software development), scheduling, or a start and a finish point.

Jan had also been anticipating changes to editorial practice and so early in 1997 had taken up postgraduate study in online education. Since the course was offered entirely online, she was finding the experience of being a student in an online learning environment a valuable addition to her understanding of the 'first student' role of editors in a distance education publishing context.

Two other editors were also working on Web-related issues: Rosemary, who was responsible for the professional development of 25 editors and was trying to develop guidelines for publishing on the Web, and Alice, who was working on a bilingual CD ROM for an external client. They were invited to become part of the group, since both had taken on challenging, difficult and fairly isolated roles.

Despite being located on two campuses in two cities (some 70 minutes drive-time apart) we five editors began meeting at the beginning of 1998. We agreed that one of the purposes of the group would be to offer professional and personal support to each other – that together we would make a safe place to talk about the challenges and difficulties inherent in managing our work and our professional lives. By April 1998:

- Rosemary and Susan were writing up the processes involved in developing and producing the first complete online unit in the Arts Faculty.
- Alice was writing about the processes, and the problems, in her CD ROM project.
- Rosemary was identifying 'content areas' for professional development workshops for the editorial group during 1998, and wondering how she could find the time to develop and deliver the workshops.
- Jan was studying Web publishing, and was exploring whether there really was a place for editors in this environment.
- She also had a course project to complete that was to be workplace-related and presented as a Web-based learning environment.
- Alison was preparing a paper comparing the traditional role of the editor in publishing with the more complex role of an editor in the distance education context, and considering some of the issues raised by a shift to publishing online in an educational context.

Other colleagues were continuing to express their worries and concerns about the way in which the editor's role might change, and were feeling anxious about the lack of guidelines and processes for managing online projects or managing materials with online components. We had formed our support group, but what were we going to do about sharing our knowledge with our broader group of colleagues, and how would we do it?

What do you see as the most important things that this group can accomplish?
How should the group work be managed?
What do you think happened next?

PART 2

'I have an idea!' offered Jan to an April meeting. 'Could we make my study project an online professional development programme for all the editorial staff? Its focus can be on editing online publications.' The group tossed the idea around, quickly realizing its potential to support Rosemary's need to undertake professional development for the whole editorial group, introduce to that group critical reflective practice and action research processes (these had become part of the conscious practice of the reference group), and offer all editorial staff the opportunity to explore the impact of the new digital technologies on their work by becoming online students themselves.

This would be a change of direction for the group, moving from group support of individual projects to undertaking one project together. We all thought the suggestion was brilliant! It would answer the needs and interests of our colleagues, and would also give us the opportunity to share our learning with the broader editorial group. We were very excited, but how would five people with different experiences and different professional backgrounds work together to develop such a creature?

As we were working across two different campuses and cities, we agreed to communicate about the project's development by using online conferencing. Getting to this point of agreement quickly threw up a number of questions:

- Could we 'teach' our colleagues and do so online? Although we had all taught in the past, in different contexts, we were not acknowledged as 'teachers' in the university. Most of us had been involved in delivering professional development for support or academic staff but online teaching and learning was very new territory and our levels of confidence varied.
- How did we really feel about using computer conferencing to talk about, track and 'archive' the developmental work? Would doing this give us practice in working collaboratively online? Some of us had recently had very unpleasant experiences in an online computer conferencing course, yet Jan's course was providing an effective and illuminating experience.
- How were we going to 'write collaboratively'?
- What were the implications of this being an 'assessable' project for Jan if others were involved in the writing?
- What was our body of knowledge, our knowledge base or 'curriculum'?
- Were there really differences in editing online and multimedia materials?

By early June 1998, we were planning and coordinating the project.

How should the group proceed?
What 'ground rules' should they establish for the project?
Do you foresee any potential areas of difficulty and conflict for the group?

PART 3

Alison dealt with the sudden and very keen interest of our divisional and executive management in the evolving programme, getting us breathing space to work by keeping them 'at bay' until we were ready to 'show and tell'. Susan kicked off the discussion about what online moderating might involve for us, and we invited Mary, an educational developer and evaluator, into the project as mentor.

A deadline for delivery at the beginning of August was suggested by Rosemary, who was keen to see some kind of professional development offered to editors by the end of the year. Jan had an initial assignment deadline of mid-July, so by mid-June we agreed that she would start drafting the text for the seven modules that comprised the programme. In doing some of the first drafts, Jan drew not only on group discussions, but also on existing materials. The module on project management drew on a paper prepared by Susan and Rosemary. Most of the module on structural editing was written by Alice and was edited and rephrased by all the group members. The module setting up the group project for participants was outlined by Jan, and reshaped and written by Alison, and almost all of the issues outlined in Alison's draft paper became part of the content of different modules.

With the time constraints and tight deadlines we'd imposed, good working relationships came under pressure. There were times of great strain as tensions developed between our different working styles and we struggled to resolve those differences and stay focused on the task we'd set ourselves.

We were not all comfortable working in the online conference. We tried synchronous chats instead of meeting face to face, but found we could not all keep up with the pauses and the faltering nature of the discussion; the frustration led us to work asynchronously. But this in itself required reading, assessing the logic and flow, commenting on and responding to large amounts of text. While some were happy with a narrative writing style, others felt more comfortable with arguments and content expressed in bullet points. And while some were happy working on screen, others required hard copy. Some of us were able to work from home with or without a printer, others had no access outside work time.

The sheer volume of the material we were writing, along with the deadlines that we had set ourselves and that were now expected of us by our colleagues and managers, heightened the pressure we were under.

We were also growing into the roles of writers and online 'teachers', a new learning experience in itself. Each draft of each module was not only read and commented on by each editor, but, given the nature of our professional backgrounds, each draft was structurally edited by each editor and copy edited by those of us who just couldn't help ourselves!

Corridor chats became a way of trying to make sense of what was happening within the group. Because of the sheer amount of work on top of our normal workloads, we could not meet together very frequently. Although we had difficulty dealing with strong emotions online, we did not find many face-to-face occasions to deal with them and they went unresolved for some time.

We were reasonably comfortable with the allocation of content modules to be written but we were not so careful allocating other tasks. For example, we didn't designate one editor as the project copy editor. This meant that managing changes and corrections became five times as large a task as it might have been.

Nor was there any detailed planning – we were being driven by the deadline and we were working reactively, almost in 'crisis mode' just to get the project completed. We found ourselves working in exactly the opposite way to the way we were advising our colleagues in the 'project management' module!

The group began as a professional development and mentoring activity for the five of us and had not seen itself as a provider of 'professional development'. Yet suddenly, we were teachers, even experts. These expectations took us well beyond our comfort zones. In hindsight this was a significant change of direction and we wondered whether the project was hijacking the reference group process and its original intention. Once the project had begun and there was a 'public' expectation, could we admit the project was too big, that there was not enough time, and that we might 'fail' our colleagues if we didn't complete?

'Ownership' and the nature of collaborative writing became an issue for us, which was never quite resolved. The way the project originated as Jan's assignment and therefore as Jan's 'idea' meant that members of the group had difficulty 'owning' the development process as a truly 'group' and collaborative one. We failed to define what we meant by 'collaborative writing'. Did we all have to write separate drafts that would be brought together into one? Was it enough for one person to prepare a draft for comment by others, and then for it to be rewritten? Individuals would make comments such as, 'but I didn't write as much' or, 'I didn't participate as much as X', and remained unconvinced that this need not obviate ownership.

There was some reluctance to 'claim' group ownership, yet there was mutual excitement and pride in what we were achieving as a group. Some of this had to do with the group's extremely strong ethics – an almost fastidious concern for not claiming credit for someone else's work.

Our collective understanding and knowledge were creating something bigger and more comprehensive than we had imagined we were capable of producing. So there were times of great exhilaration and joy; our confidence grew, and we began to appreciate and value our differences. Then the development and design were done, and the project was ready to be launched and delivered to our colleagues – and all this in a very intense five weeks.

The project was duly launched and delivered. The key teaching and learning issues that arose from the programme and the participants' and moderators' experiences are another story in themselves. Suffice it to say that throughout the evaluation, which we carried out over several months following the project's completion, responses from our colleagues were very positive. Participants were encouraged to critique the Web site which contained the main teaching material and reflect on how the FirstClass conference space was working as a teaching/learning medium, and changes were incorporated wherever possible in response to colleagues' comments and suggestions. But we found that the most heartening response was an increase in confidence and a sense of excitement in dealing with online technologies, where previously there had been anxiety and uncertainty.

How successful do you consider the process to have been?
Could any of the difficulties have been avoided?
Are there any implications for your own work that can be taken from this project?

CASE REPORTERS' DISCUSSION

So, from our beginnings as a reference group to support our work and develop some guidelines for working with online technologies, very quickly our roles changed to ones of course developers, writers and teachers, and evaluators. These were roles that 'belonged' to academic or professional development staff. But we, too, had a body of knowledge and changing paradigms within it to explore with our colleagues. The demands of naming existing knowledge, outlining questions about how it might change and structuring this into an online learning environment made us reflect on our knowledge-base *and* how it might best be taught online – as those responsible for curriculum development and online delivery in any area of knowledge must do.

Our immediate managers had supported our move into the course developer/teacher role. Our collaborative/team approach to developing and writing the online programme and our uses of computer-mediated communication (CMC), came to be acknowledged as providing a model or exemplar for teaching staff developing online teaching and learning environments.

But our experience as 'course developers' seemed the very opposite of the institution's implied position that individual academics should be responsible for writing, producing and delivering their own course materials. It reinforced a long-held position in distance education: that a team-based, collaborative approach to course development offers far more potential for a quality outcome. It also confirmed the view that writing and course production are two quite different processes. Online self-publishing is appropriate for an individual's own work or their own Web page, but producing course materials with an institution's imprimatur requires quality control at the writing stage, as well as at the production stage. The more diverse the offerings an institution wishes to offer, the more the need for multiple quality checks.

Our experience was that time for planning is crucial. While simplifying some of the delivery processes, online technologies invite more complex content. Text, audio, video and images can be combined and delivered in one place. Different media can interrogate each other, not only enriching the learning environment, but enhancing learner participation and interactivity.

The project also raised further critical questions regarding our future editing role. For example, is it more important to focus on site mapping, structure and navigation and seamless integration of CMC – the very architecture of the learning environment – than on the integration of graphics into an individual Web page, or on ensuring textual material is error-free?

We learnt that developing materials for online delivery required 'front-end' structuring. For the online 'reader', becoming 'lost in cyberspace' is tantamount to abandonment: there may be no book to go back to, no first page to touch and turn again. The editor's expertise in 'structural editing' takes on new significance in online/multimedia and needs to be aligned with the educational designer's emphasis on sequencing and synthesizing a knowledge base. In print-based materials an absence of either or both might not compromise learning, but online the risks of creating confusion are much greater.

Within the scope of the editorial role we found ourselves rethinking much conventional practice, for instance:

- *Consistency*: if there is consistency in a page template design, in placement of navigational tools and menus across site pages, does it matter if there is inconsistency in text-based headings and textual matter?
- *Style of writing*: the medium seems best to support writing that is brief, not discursive. Should we be producing such text and reworking the writing of others?
- *Emphasis*: in print, emphasis is usually indicated by the use of italics. Onscreen italics blur. What house style might we evolve to add emphasis in text? Use of colour, use of bold?

Given the complexities of the process in developing learning materials for an online environment and all that we learnt from taking on new roles for the staff development project, it's clear that the boundaries between editors, writers, producers and project managers are not clear-cut, and professional roles are changing.

The institutional vision remains that academic staff will individually and in course teams develop, produce and deliver their own online materials, with less centrally offered support. The introduction and rolling out of an instructional management system (IMS) with graphic interface, will allow academic staff not only to 'manage' the administration of their courses, but also to put learning material into an interface with basic preset instructional and graphic design.

Since we began writing, new positions have been introduced reflecting the complexity of the editorial role as it will need to evolve to respond to the introduction of online teaching, learning and publishing technologies.

There is institutional recognition of the need for more support to faculty staff at the development phase of online and multimedia learning environments, the 'front end', the educational design, shaping and structuring of materials, rather than at the 'back end' of production. This is coupled with an increased institutional emphasis on a coherent pedagogical approach to incorporating online technologies into whole programme development. But these resources are directed towards strategically chosen programmes that enhance the institution's reputation for appropriate, competitive and quality delivery.

Editors' expertise in and knowledge of course materials development, their experience in working closely with academic staff and in being often on the front line in perceiving academic professional development needs, their understanding of the need for the effective integration of materials in all media, coupled with skills in structuring materials and undertaking complex project management, have seen some take up roles as 'programme/project developers' to work solely at the 'front-end' with educational designers. Others have had their organizational and scheduling expertise channelled into faculty liaison positions to ensure that planning and delivery are implemented effectively. While editing textual material to be produced for any medium continues at the university it does so increasingly as a process of 'value-adding' in strategic and targeted areas.

Given the territorial raids across traditional professional borders that are continuing, was the experience of producing our own staff development project for a professional group, which now no longer exists as such, worthwhile? We think so. Travelling without maps and charting new professional terrain may have been difficult at the time, but the knowledge, understanding and insights gained continue to inform our professional practice in the digital age.

CHAPTER 18

TECHNO HERO FIASCO

Case reporters: Julianne Moss, Mary Fearnley-Sander and Claire Hiller

Issues raised

This case concerns problems that arise when the introduction of online teaching is policy-led with little prior thought given to operational consequences.

Background

This case study involves the development of an online teacher education programme. The case has its origins in 1997 when a newly formed multi-campus university (with campuses separated by 250 kilometres of highway) introduced a two-year graduate pre-service teacher programme. University and faculty strategic plans demanded that the course be available online, and development and implementation of the course were the responsibility of the three authors.

PART 1

Semester one, 1999. It was our first experience of developing and teaching a flexibly delivered course, and it was not going well. We'd had trouble getting the course prepared in time, and the technology (associated with both the video lectures and the course Web site) was letting us down. For example, in the very first video lecture the audio failed, and in the second week, there was no contact at all. Equally alarming problems also emerged in the online environment.

Not surprisingly, the dominant reaction of the students was one of resistance. They were concerned about lack of access to computers, lack of skills to access course materials and lecturers, the desire to have more face-to-face contact with staff and their need to know the 'right' answer, rather than explore the openness of the course as intended.

Early in the semester, an e-mail from a student concerned about assessment and other learning issues was replied to as follows:

> I will discuss the assignment with all the group in much more detail as we go. There is no need to be anxious about it at the moment. As you learn more about the course you will begin to see more clearly what we are doing. You are not expected to know the answers now as this is considered part of your learning. In your course outline there are some references that are in the library and which might help. You do not need to read all of them but have a browse and see what might be possibilities. Do not worry, you will not be disadvantaged in any way. There is no right answer, there are a range of responses all of which are equally valid. The assignment is seeking your own experience and allows the possibility of applying that to the learning of your future students.

Despite the reassurance and openness of our responses, student complaints and feelings of injustice and loss of access to learning continually beset us. As one student wrote in an e-mail in early April, eight weeks into the semester:

> This is an issue of equity of access which students are concerned about. With the inherent difficulty of receiving the course via video link in the first place i.e. not having face to face contact, communication being difficult and limited time to question the lecturer regarding meanings, we would like this issue addressed and some exploration provided of why this is occurring and how this is impacting on us as learners.

Acknowledgment of the difficulties did little to allay anxieties and tensions. A reply to the above e-mail said:

> It is the policy of the Faculty of Education to deliver these courses by video and staff are doing their best to deliver as well as they can given the circumstances. We would prefer face-to-face teaching but this is not possible at the moment within the constraints of staffing and budgeting. If you do not get to ask your questions, I encourage you to e-mail the lecturer concerned. It is part of University and Faculty strategic plans to move to all kinds of flexible delivery. It is also part of the state Department of Education plan to do professional development online, so we can expect more of it in the future, not less. I realize that this can be frustrating to you all, as well as to us, but we will continue to try to do our best.

Unfortunately this did little to improve staff–student relationships or to enhance a supportive and open learning community. We as staff intended to encourage a discourse of openness, a move towards cooperation and negotiation among students, and a move away from a discourse of competitiveness. But while we encouraged openness, the students demanded closure. Student resistance led to complaints to the Student Union and Head of School. As a result, at the end of semester one, the ongoing saga reached a climax and we 'techno heroes' were brought before a meeting of the Faculty Executive, the staff, a Student Union representative and students.

What is going on here?
What do you see as the principal concerns of the students and of the staff?
What do you think was the outcome of the meeting?

PART 2

We were annihilated, clearly demonstrating the power of student resistance and a predictable lack of support for those of us who had constructed the programme. The meeting resulted in considerable changes to the use of the online programme and to assessment procedures. The log of policy and events, shown in Table 18.1, provides a vivid contrast between the policy intention and the actuality.

The log reveals the situation in which we were caught, and demonstrates the interrelationships of discourse, pedagogy and subjectivity. Our aim in producing the log was to convey the contrast that existed between the externally produced strategic direction and the reality of trying to implement and make this work on the ground. For us it is a story of technical fiascos, student resistance, staff grandstanding and appeasement.

The open-ended feedback provided in the SETL (Student Evaluation of Teaching and Learning) completed at the end of the academic year in October 1999, raised further questions surrounding the construction of teaching and learning that our future teachers were developing. Some of the comments included:

- Found group work onerous in the extreme. It's not fair to have to work with uncommitted people and then have your marks dragged down.
- Group work is highly irrelevant as it is very difficult to find time to work together due to pracs and lack of contact time together – we each have other commitments and group work imposes on these.
- The way this course is assessed needs to be altered. Group assessment is useful but not as a major part of the unit.
- The online assessment and readings were a waste of time and didn't work. Meeting face to face seemed more productive.
- It was a pity we couldn't have more classes as they were great classes – just hard to remember because of the gaps.
- We're drama students so we don't use e-mail.
- Inequity – limited time to question the lecturer regarding meanings.
- Apart from e-mail very hard to consult lecturers.

Table 18.1   Log of policy and events

Policy texts	Log
University plan 1999–2001 The university will… aim to be more accessible by adopting the best teaching methods, based where appropriate on the best available technologies (page 7)	1. The Faculty Strategic plan commits us to teaching our course on the other campus in 1999. No extra funds. We can bid for funds from teaching grants to convert our courses to flexible/online delivery. 2. Nov. 1998. We get grants ($5,000 each). We plan for integrating the curriculum, building a virtual classroom, upgrading our skills.
Wide access to general education *Outcome* Students have improved access to a general education in the sciences, arts and commerce, offered at a competitive national standard *Outputs…* • Development of a plan and implementation schedule by the teaching and learning committee during 1999, for the flexible delivery of programs (page 11)	3. Jan 1999. We hand over online design to commercial developers. We can't do it ourselves in the time available. 4. First term Week 1: Audio fails in mass video lecture. 5. Friday: The students are bussed down from the other campus for training in online services. The server is down. 6. Week 2: Second online training day with students from the north. Computers freeze when students practice chat sessions in the labs. 7. Week 2: Video lecture. No contact at all. 8. Our site is ready but navigation problems make it incoherent.
IT and the future of the university *Outcome* Effective and efficient use of IT to enhance the University's teaching…	9. Week 3: Students complain to their union and to our head dept. Complaints about e-mail access, discussion groups, navigation, difficulties downloading course material. The labs on one campus only have Netscape 2. Outcome: the first work task will not be counted in student marks. 10. Weeks 3–11. No successful video connections so far to large lecture theatre. Student difficulties with site continue.
Faculty of Education 1998–2000 Strategic plan *Key Result Areas…* 3.3 Increase use of flexible delivery in teaching and course delivery in at least 2 units by end of 1999 and 3 by end of 2000. $0.5 million IT upgrade Increased involvement in school-based PD cross-campus delivery	11. Week 12. The first successful video lecture! But distance students said they felt excluded. 12. Semester Break. Faculty Executive hearing of student complaints about the course. Meeting addressed by representatives of the students and attended by Student Union reps. Student demands: replace the online and distance components with face to face (through block teaching); end perceived discrimination against distance students. Team to report to Executive Dean on follow-up. 13. Semester 2: Commercial providers are no longer accessible to staff.

Table 18.1   *continued*

14.	December: E-mail from technician: 'Since Tuesday, while carrying out backups on the [southern server] a hard disk failed… The 2.1Gb drive appears to have failed due to overheating of the casing that it was in. The overheating was so extreme that the rubber feet of the casing melted away… The backup tapes were taken to [the north] but the best efforts to recover the data failed.'

Fundamentally, we felt that our problem was the introduction of ICT at this time, in the way we chose to develop the course (due to limited time) and was a consequence of university policy. This policy was not a choice made by the staff, nor a response to the expressed needs of students. It has raised many questions for us, which are likely also the concerns of others. The questions continue to inform our process of reflection and action on the events.

What do you think were the main factors contributing to the difficulties outlined in this case?
How could these difficulties have been avoided?
How should the decision to implement ICT in a course be reached?
Do the experiences described in this case have repercussions for your own teaching?

CASE REPORTERS' DISCUSSION

The complaints of the students on the student evaluations were all provoked by the features of the course that came out of our construction of the way teachers should be prepared: the time spent on group work, the interaction of students with learning and with each other, the emphasis on independent learning and the making of multiple meanings. What we encountered was a technological solution that effectively precluded the educational solution we preferred. The SETL statements are taken as incontestable measures of performance. They are the means by which the institution allocates departmental funding.

What view of the preparation of teachers makes these features deficits? Posing this question makes us realize that the course has a meaning to students other than its meaning as curriculum. Activities that frustrate or jeopardize the market value of the course, raised by the individual student's labour input, are perceived as defects. These are defects of design, that is, defects in what a teacher education course should be in its aims and outcomes. The coherence of the course is the extent to which its assessment and workload strategies converge on individually appropriated awards.

One of the most notable features of the interactions over this course is the asymmetry of problems and solutions. The log details the failure of technology: only two lectures were successfully delivered all semester; the online component was withdrawn mid-year; the year ended with technical burlesque – a meltdown of the course right down to its rubber feet. The journal record of the climactic event – the Faculty Executive hearing – details hardware and software access as the substantive problems. The dilemma the university faced in needing to do more with fewer staff seemed to create an opportunity: an opportunity for us to 'show willing' and at the same time position us to operate in the new environment.

By being techno heroes we could enhance our position in the faculty programme. We could alter the conditions of our work in the future, using flexible delivery to create more time for work – for research. We could make our teaching our research! At the least we could protect the programme on 'our' campus and our jobs with it.

We saw the opportunity to create a course that exemplified and implemented our theories of teaching and learning and so to affirm our professional identities. That priority was reflected in our ideals of curriculum integration, the multi-dimensionality of teaching practice and the indeterminacy of learning. We envisioned the site as a virtual classroom: the material (videoed practice, work samples, problem-framing text and research perspectives) presented archivally, linked by different, equally statused navigational tracks and avoiding the segregation of the educational disciplines. Learning was to be activated by group collaboration in an environment that might exist among real school staff. It was to be problem-based learning, with no teacher to read for clues, no determinate solutions.

We had made a product in our own image and paradoxically replicated the academic curriculum's exclusion of the learner. We had not used our planning time to find out what know-how and training our students required to make the technologies of flexible learning work. Nor had we understood what would be required to ensure the technologies worked in the infrastructural context of our institution. As a result, we made assumptions about the technological skills of our postgraduate cohort of students that proved to be wrong. We did not develop competence in our own Web page design so that we could monitor the construction of the navigation of our virtual classroom. We consigned the conversion of our ideas of a Web design to commercial designers as a subordinate technical task. The result was that our ideas were embedded in an implementation fundamentally at odds with the logic of the commercial design. This outcome was partly the consequence of the nature of the courseware, in which interactivity mainly meant surveillance of student work patterns, and test scores quantified learning.

In the face of the collapse of the technical solution, the decisions were to return to conventional teaching and to abandon the model of learning implied in the idea of a virtual classroom. On top of that came the shaming of the staff in institutional forums of complaint – the calling of the Faculty Executive forum itself and the institutional evaluations of staff performance as teachers. These evaluations contained no mention of the technical problems. What earned the staff opprobrium was their course.

Why were the technological failures protected from critique? A reason suggests itself partly through the way that we ourselves defended our course. We were curiously complicit in this protection of technology. We justified the use of distance learning technologies in political terms, not in educational ones: as university and faculty policy, and coercively, as the new order of things. This was a political defence, because it gave us leverage on student compliance. And the students used the same coin. If technology was the new order of things, their professional competence was vulnerable to attack were they to resist it. If, by contrast, the grounds of dissatisfaction were related to their learning disadvantage, politically the university could not afford to exact their compliance.

We believe that our narrative has value for those caught in technology-based change brought on by university exigencies rather than educational innovations. For us the exercise has been liberating. It has provided us with the opportunity for reflection on our role and the nature of our work. Practically it has had valuable outcomes for us as well. The decision to teach cross-campus has reinstated face-to-face teaching and so has meant that we have the space to create the programme, emancipated from the straitjacket of commercial software. The outcome is control of our own provision and greater institutional realism about the feasibility of technology as a solution to educational problems.

CHAPTER 19

THE TRAGEDY OF THE EARLY ADOPTERS

Case reporters: Mark Smithers and Christine Spratt

Issues raised

This case explores the complexities associated with introducing innovation in a university, using a fictional example. In particular, the case examines the personal, professional and organizational implications of an early commitment to promoting the use of innovative technology in teaching and learning.

Background

Riverview is a dual-mode university, having both on-campus and distance students and being actively committed to the development of flexible programmes. Peter is an academic in a teaching department. The Riverview Flexible Learning Division (RFLD) is a small central unit providing services related to teaching and educational technology. The story spans a five-year period.

PART 1

Peter was in a quandary. He had come to realize that he had been teaching the same subjects for 10 years under mounting pressure, to increasing numbers of generally uninterested students with whom he spent less time working in small groups. He also realized that he did not have the time to create the high-quality online teaching and learning material that he knew could be used to facilitate learning. 'Just how did it come to this?' mused Peter. 'What on earth should I do?'

Peter had come to Riverview University in 1995 after teaching 'built environment' for five years at Welshpool Polytechnic and New Midlands University. Those years had been dominated by course and curriculum development, rigorous validation procedures and equally rigorous accreditation by external professional bodies. During that time, Peter had developed an interest in and commitment to learning through simulation, using problem-based learning in the context of 'real' building projects and working with students in small groups. Prior to leaving New Midlands University, he started to use the Internet for information gathering and professional communication. He began to see the possibilities of providing learning experiences that were accessible at any time or place for his students.

When he joined Riverview University, a recent course restructure left Peter temporarily with a minimal teaching load. This provided an opportunity to experiment with the Internet. He set up his own Web server and proceeded to create basic Web sites containing his course material.

He immediately appreciated the enormous potential of the new technologies for teaching and learning and attempted to raise discussion about this potential at meetings and with his academic colleagues. Initially, he was met with guarded interest by some and polite indifference by others. Over a period of time, some staff became curious while others became openly antagonistic. When he suggested using the Web as a way of displaying students' work and demonstrating that the school was a vibrant dynamic place, antagonism became resistance. However, he did receive some support from the Head of School and subsequently the Dean of the Faculty.

A year after arriving at Riverview, Peter became involved with the RFLD, a small group comprising a professional development team and a software development team.

RFLD approached Peter's school and offered to assist in setting up a high-powered school-based Web server for the development of online teaching and learning materials. Peter was nominated as the appropriate person to work with the software development team in procuring, installing and configuring the Web server. This was despite the fact that other staff in the school taught courses within its information technology (IT) curriculum and Peter did not. His nomination caused some bitterness among those who had IT responsibilities in the school and their colleagues.

Peter started to develop strategies to integrate Web-based learning into his courses, all of which were for full-time, on-campus students in years one and two. His first strategy involved gradually creating online content that supplemented his lectures. He intended that the content would not be text driven but would contain interactive components that would enhance students' understanding of principles or key concepts. Peter had been concerned for many years that his students, generally immature undergraduates, were passive learners sitting unresponsively in large lecture groups. He recognized that he was not a natural 'show person': he was concerned that the message in his teaching was being lost and that the students' learning was not as enjoyable as it could be. His idea was to give fewer lectures and that they would be keynote in nature rather than delivering routine information. He intended that his students would supplement these with interactive online learning, tutorials (with Peter or a tutor), paper-based readers and practical workshops. He selected each method of delivery carefully for its strengths as a teaching and learning strategy.

Second, he planned to create a Web-based simulation for his problem-based learning course that would see the Web used as a virtual office at which students could check in to become involved in interacting with a simulated environment where messages from clients, contractors and others would be held. These in turn would dictate short, medium and long-term goals for the student groups.

His third strategy was to encourage students to contribute to their own learning using the Internet as the vehicle for collaboration. Peter did this by setting a major assignment that the students had to submit electronically through a browser interface. The students had to provide a unique submission consisting of a computer-generated drawing or set of photographs and accompanied by a detailed commentary broken down into a series of fields. All of this information was stored in a database that could then be searched by other students after the submissions had been made. This was Peter's first step towards creating an innovative online information repository that could be used by students in subsequent years and in other courses.

While the repository operated successfully for two years, problems arose with his other strategies. An application for funding for the Web-based simulation failed. Furthermore, Peter realized that the time taken to complete the necessary interactive components, even at low interactivity levels, was more than he had available.

During this period the antagonism of his colleagues grew. There were those who resisted using the computer for learning and resented Riverview's increasing and explicit rhetoric encouraging the adoption of new technologies. Colleagues openly criticized Peter in front of students. Some resented his role in managing the school server and eventually succeeded in having him replaced.

Over the next two years Peter's colleagues gradually marginalized him and he became increasingly depressed. His application for a faculty teaching and learning award was unsuccessful and the time devoted to developing online teaching and learning material meant that his PhD studies and his research output fell away. The last straw for Peter was the arrival of a new and powerful senior academic within the school, who Peter saw as taking credit for his work and appointing himself to key faculty committees for which Peter had originally been nominated. Peter was at a crossroads in his career. What was he to do?

What do you think is going on here?
What advice would you give Peter?
What do you think happened next?

PART 2

It was a tough decision. Four years after joining Riverview as an academic staff member Peter resigned from his department and accepted a job at a substantially lower salary as a software developer with the RFLD. He felt that he had reached a dead end within the faculty and that he could pursue his interest in Internet-based teaching and contribute more to the university's online teaching and learning initiatives by working as a full-time Web developer in partnership with academic staff. Peter had come to the realization that expecting academic staff to develop their own online teaching and learning material was both unrealistic and unreasonable. He estimated that only a small proportion of the academic population would be interested in producing their own material and an even smaller number would be able to cope with the increasingly complex demands of Web development. A preferable model would see academic staff working with educational software developers to produce high-quality teaching and learning material. Having seen the work of the RFLD, Peter decided that he would prefer to use his skill and experience working within that group.

RFLD was formed in the same year that Peter arrived at Riverview and their experience can be seen as an organizational corollary of his experience. Under visionary leadership RFLD realized, very early, the impact of the Internet for teaching and learning and started to move towards the development of online material. In the face of inertia from Riverview's IT division, RFLD set up a second university Web server and provided space and access for academics and other divisions to publish online material. High-level Web and multimedia teaching and learning material continued to be produced by RFLD and the software team in particular.

During 1996 the software team created some of the earliest mainstream database-driven Web sites in the world. In 1997 members of the software team proposed a flexible integrated online learning environment that would have ensured Riverview was at the cutting edge of educational technology delivery in the tertiary sector, rather than becoming a mainstream follower. For two years RFLD sought access to the university's student information database so that they could create a personalized student information portal (as had UCLA, using the same technologies). Team members developed prototype online evaluation systems, discussion and collaboration systems and school online information systems.

However, during the last two years RFLD had become increasingly marginalized as other groups within the university started to appreciate the importance of the Internet. RFLD's role as innovation champion was challenged as two other groups within the university created Web development teams offering development services to teaching and administrative units within the university. These units then attempted to compete aggressively for the work that RFLD was carrying out for faculty-based clients. Senior management started to realize the importance of the Internet for teaching and learning and actively encouraged the location of development work within the IT division. Following Peter's earlier experience, RFLD had been an early innovator that now found itself increasingly marginalized and approaching a crossroad.

What factors do you think contributed to the change in RFLD's circumstances?
What would be your advice to RFLD?
What do you think actually happened next?

PART 3

In order to lead, and perhaps fearful of the potential costs of proliferating high-quality developments, the university executive needed to find a solution that it perceived would make it easy for faculties to put their courses online with the minimum of fuss. They found this by searching for an appropriate enterprise-level instructional management system (IMS), which quickly became promoted as the needed panacea.

Once the decision was made to commit to a particular IMS a number of staff were told not to comment negatively on the choice. To staff, such apparent coercion reflected both the ineptitude of the executive in managing the university's technology agenda and the lack of intelligent, critical debate surrounding these important issues.

Soon after, the head of the software team left and, in an unrelated move, the university announced that it was creating a new organization that would involve merging RFLD with the much larger traditional print publishing group within the university.

With the creation of the new division, there was an increasing emphasis on *procuring* digital teaching and learning material with grudging references to the university's intention to 'if necessary *develop*' educational technology solutions; reference to 'development activity' later disappeared completely. It appeared that Riverview University was content to be a follower rather than a leader in this increasingly volatile and competitive field.

From the RFLD's perspective, its innovative work had been destroyed and Peter and the other software developers left the university. An opportunity to grasp the technological agenda firmly and move forward into new and exciting ways of practice by supporting a small group of dedicated, multi-skilled developers was lost. As one faculty IT manager stated, Riverview has 'effectively stripped itself of the capacity to be innovative at a time in higher education when innovation is everything'.

What do you think are the major factors that contributed to this outcome?
What alternative actions or approaches could Peter and the RFLD have taken?
What do you think were the primary motivations of the university executive management?
Have you seen or experienced a similar series of events yourself?

CASE REPORTERS' DISCUSSION

Peter's story and that of the RFLD raise complex issues about the nature of academic work, about universities as 'learning organizations', and the way in which innovators and innovations can or should be managed and supported to be institutional leaders. We can partially address these issues by fore-grounding key questions that we believe the case raises.

First, why does teaching excellence continue to be marginalized in tertiary education? Contemporary innovative thinking about tertiary education is embedded in models of learning that destroy the notion of knowledge as a commodity and promote knowledge as a critical and collaborative interactive process of meaning making. The aim is to offer learners opportunities and experiences that will help them become autonomous lifelong learners, capable of problem solving and critical thinking and which move them from being passive learners to active participants in their own learning.

Peter's practice reflected these beliefs, and so too did the collective work of the RFLD. Interestingly, those areas of the university with whom RFLD collaborated recognized the great contribution that it had made over time in improving teaching and learning with technology. However, those who felt that the university was expending resources unnecessarily or who could be described as 'technophobic' were content to see its demise. Organizational cultural change does not happen rapidly; however, the experience at Riverview reflected in this case demonstrates the damage that can occur when executive-level management has a rhetorical commitment to such change, little understanding of operational issues and is not prepared to trust those with demonstrated expertise in the field to lead.

Second, how can universities become innovative learning organizations and succeed in an increasingly competitive and volatile educational environment? In his study of five European universities, Clark (1998, p xiv) contends that 'complexity and uncertainty [is] now endemic [in tertiary education], no one knows with any degree of confidence what the twenty-first century holds in store for universities'. He goes on to suggest that the only means by which universities can hope to excel, indeed survive, is to 'learn from efforts to innovate in the overall character of universities' (p xiv).

Universities are, generally speaking, conservative organizations. Innovations such as those described in this case are seen covertly by such organizations as 'risky practices'. Where research output, costs, resource limitations and student outcomes drive the agenda of schools and faculties within universities, risk-taking behaviour in such highly bureaucratic and process-oriented environments is perceived as dangerous.

Third, how can universities work best to place educational technology development central to innovative curriculum design? In a comprehensive evaluation of the success of IT projects in Australian higher education, Alexander, McKenzie and Geissenger (1998) investigated the ways in which the use of IT in universities may benefit student learning. The study reviewed over 150 technology projects that received funding from the (federally funded) Committee for the Advancement of University Teaching over a two-year period. They highlight the complexities of technology development in higher education when they state that:

> while much of the early development of information technology projects has been the work of the enthusiastic experimenter, significant educational software development has become a professional and multi-faceted activity, requiring the interplay of expertise in learning design, project management, financial management, interpersonal skills, programming, graphic design, media digitisation and evaluation. (p 256)

Writing from a North American perspective, Gilbert (2000), argues that:

> At most colleges and universities the supply of resources available to help faculty improve teaching and learning with technology is simply inadequate to meet rising expectations. In addition, these resources are usually not well coordinated – wasteful duplication is too common. The usual lack of coordination and collaboration among different parts of most educational institutions compounds the impact of the shortage of support service professionals and undermines the college's or university's capacity to adopt and adapt valuable new combinations of technology, pedagogy, and educational purpose. These combinations can only be developed and used effectively if the essential expertise and resources controlled by the 'Constituencies for Change' can be focused TOGETHER on improving teaching and learning.

Gilbert's 'Constituencies for Change', 'are those who must be involved in a coherent, continuing cost-effective effort to improve teaching and learning with technology'. According to Gilbert, key members of this group are those he calls 'compassionate pioneers' and whom others have called 'early adopters' (Rogers, 1995). Gilbert writes elegantly of these people:

> At any college or university, Compassionate Pioneers are both a valuable and scarce resource. As others discover the skills, expertise, and availability of these special people, requests for their help can multiply rapidly. Compassionate

> Pioneers need to be honored, protected, and supported before they simply wear out and begin to avoid the questions and resent the solicitations of their colleagues.

Peter (along with his colleagues in the RFLD) was one of Gilbert's 'compassionate pioneers'. He was one of Alexander *et al*'s (1998, p 257) 'enthusiastic experimenters' and an 'early adopter'. Peter found his teaching repertoire extended by the adoption of new technologies and he found the experience intrinsically, intellectually and personally rewarding. Yet he was unsupported and marginalized by his colleagues. His move to the more 'cosmopolite' group (Rogers, 1995) could have heralded a period of professional growth for himself and the contribution he could have made to the RFLD. Yet we see the outcome of his experience in the RFLD. Perhaps Riverview University should heed Gilbert's belief:

> We need a new kind of Vision Worth Working Toward – a vision that embraces change, sets a direction for the integration of new applications of technology, makes the most of the resources we've already got, and recognizes how important it is to choose a future based on realistic analysis of where we are, where we've been, and where we want to go.

Like Weil (1999), we believe that in the context of higher education 'we do live in an unstable state and no nostalgic account of higher education will bring anything remotely stable back into being'. In this story we see Peter and the RFLD recognizing the chaos and dynamism of the contemporary higher education sector bought on by the revolution in information technology. We see them moving to adapt their practices to such change. Moreover, as evidenced by the strategies management took to restructure the RFLD in this story, we also argue that traditional universities seek change strategies that are managed and implemented by elitist administrators who, according to Weil (1999, p 1) impose 'structural solutions to complex problems that are by no means structural in nature'. This allows little possibility of generating 'the risk taking that is integral to maintaining a responsive and innovative system' (p 22).

References

Alexander, S, McKenzie, J and Geissenger, H (1998) *An Evaluation of Information Technology Projects for University Learning*, Committee for University Teaching and Learning, Department of Employment and Education, Training and Youth Affairs, Canberra, Australia

Clark, B (1998) *Creating Entrepreneurial Universities: Organizational pathways of transformation*, International Association of Universities Press and Pergamon, Oxford

Gilbert, S (2000) 'A New Vision Worth Working Toward – Connected education and collaborative change' (www.tltgroup.org/gilbert/NewVwwt2000-2-14-00.htm)

Rogers, E (1995) *Diffusion of Innovations*, 4th edn, Free Press, New York

Weil, S (1999) 'Recreating universities for beyond the stable state: From "Dearingesque" systemic control to post-Dearing systemic learning and inquiry', *Systems Research and Behavioural Science*, **16**, 2 (www.epub.med.iacnet.com)

CONCLUSION

Reflecting on the case studies and their corresponding discussions, a number of themes emerge. Overwhelmingly it would seem that despite the focus on technology, most of the issues with which the case reporters wrestled were concerned with people, their actions, interactions, collaboration (or lack of same) and achievements, as they strive to improve their teaching and their students' learning. While the introduction or insertion of technology in teaching and learning in higher education means significant change, this change in itself can mask the fact that less has changed than we might be tempted to think. As organizations, universities have characteristic ways of incorporating and resisting new forms of practice, and it is these familiar narratives that tend to recur. This closing chapter briefly draws together some of these themes and examines emerging patterns.

PLANNING AND TEAMWORK

While good planning is essential in all teaching, the requirement is amplified when new technologies are involved. The need for detailed planning is evident in the case studies, *Do We Really Need an Online Discussion Group?*, *Houston, We Have a Problem!*, *Try, Try Again!* and *Credit Where It's Due*, and it is clear that good planning not only leads to a well-integrated teaching and learning environment, but also creates a readiness to adjust the subject or course when problems arise. Planned evaluation is also a feature of the cases, and helps the course team to improve its course either immediately (*It Seemed Like a Good Idea at the Time*) or in subsequent iterations (*Try, Try Again!*).

However well planned a project is, success is highly dependent on how well the people involved can work together. Good teamwork is evident in *Do We Really Need an Online Discussion Group?*, *Credit Where It's Due* and *The Reluctant Software Developers*, while the case outline presented in *The Great Courseware Gamble* shows how teamwork can founder, especially when working groups are dispersed and when different agendas are not openly discussed and different priorities are left unresolved. *Techno Hero Fiasco* shows how a team of teachers can emerge positively from a highly negative experience, perceiving something good from a project that saw them take the blame for problems that were mostly technological in nature.

INNOVATION

Teaching online and the application of other computer-based learning approaches can involve taking risks and pushing the boundaries with respect to applications of new and emerging technologies. While some innovations are modest – *It Seemed Like a Good Idea at the Time* and *The Reluctant Software Developers* – others are much more ambitious, and can carry the burden of significant expectations, both institutionally and from government or other sponsoring agencies. This can create tensions, often from confused or competing aims – *Who Is Leading Whom?* and *The Great Courseware Gamble* – which can lead, as with the latter case, to failure.

LISTENING TO STUDENTS

The value of listening to students is apparent in most of the cases, with evaluation featuring strongly as part of the iterative cycle of development. Student feedback in *Do Students Really Want to Interact?* and *Do We Really Need an Online Discussion Group?* helped the case reporters to realign their assumptions about student interaction. Perhaps even more important, especially when developing online and other computer-based forms of teaching, is the need to involve students in development as soon as possible. Part of the reason for the ultimate success of the projects described in *Try, Try Again!* and *Poetic Seeing* was that feedback from students was sought during the developmental stages.

Being open to student criticism and responding to it is also part of 'listening'. The author of *Credit Where It's Due* had to rethink assessment policy and criteria in the light of the reactions of his students. Similarly, *It Seemed Like a Good Idea at the Time* illustrates how the quick actions of the online teacher can overcome negative student reactions to an innovative online activity.

MODERATING SKILLS

There is clearly an onus on online teachers to be vigilant in their role as moderator of group discussions. Just as the classroom tutor does not typically leave the students completely to their own devices, so the online tutor has obligations and responsibilities to ensure that the discussion is cordial, constructive and (usually!) collaborative. *Flame War* illustrates well how quickly conflict can escalate without intervention, and shows just how much time and effort are then required to set matters right. Equally, *Pacific Mayday: Conviviality Overboard* provides a surprising lesson for course organizers who had made assumptions about the expected interactions of two groups of seemingly similar students.

Moderating skills can also be required in simply getting a discussion group going, as the authors of *Do We Really Need an Online Discussion Group?* discovered to their dismay. Yes, there are examples of students getting on with learning through an online discussion group without the intervention of the teacher, as observed by the academic in *Teaching Online... Reluctantly*, but for the most part such groups require skilled and sensitive moderation. This emerged as a key issue in *Houston, We Have a Problem!* and *Credit Where It's Due*, both of which involve teachers working with small groups in online environments, coping with problems of project work and assessment.

STAFF DEVELOPMENT AND INSTITUTIONAL SUPPORT

The introduction of a new technology or approach to teaching always has staff development implications, and this is apparent in a number of the cases. *'I Have Some Pages Up!'* details the efforts of an academic staff development unit in assisting staff 'going online'. Interestingly, their action was not the result of institutional strategy, but a reaction to a seeming lack of institutional support for teaching staff. A similar motivation for action is present in both *Travelling Without Maps* and *The Tragedy of the Early Adopters*, with negative outcomes in the latter case as the institutional leaders belatedly responded to emerging problems.

TECHNOLOGICAL DEFICIENCY AND FAILURE

Perhaps surprisingly, few case study reporters focused on either deficiencies or failure in the technology with which they were trying to teach. And even when there was failure, their concerns were more with people than with machinery or software and its vagaries.

Techno Hero Fiasco illustrates this well. In this case, a group of teachers tries valiantly to overcome unrealistic development time, the failure of equipment and systems and the collapse of technological support. The reaction of the institution is also instructive. The problem is perceived as the failure of the teachers, while the failure of the technology is conveniently ignored. In *Of Heaven and Hell* the teacher wrestles with significantly 'less than perfect' videoconferencing technology. Simply keeping up with technology, especially when teaching computing, can also be an issue, well illustrated in *From Mouldy Disks to Online Fix*.

SUMMARY

Overall, the case studies reveal a range of issues, problems and concerns, many of which are well known within higher education practice. The overall message is clear – it is the ability of people to work together collaboratively and cooperatively, to treat their students with consideration and respect, and to see that for them learning is a journey that is often high risk and littered with obstacles, that underpin success in teaching. Perhaps less obviously, as with any teaching innovation, this requires the confidence to experiment. We hope that the case studies in this book cause you to think and reflect as you consider your own next steps in the development of technology-informed teaching.

FURTHER READING

Abbey, B (ed) (2000) *Instructional and Cognitive Impacts of Web-based Education*, Idea Group Publishing, Hershey, USA

Aggarwal, A (2000) *Web-Based Learning and Teaching Technologies: Opportunities and challenges*, Idea Group Publishing, Hershey, USA

Alexander, S and McKenzie, J (1998) *An Evaluation of Information Technology Projects for University Learning*, Committee for University Teaching and Staff Development, AGPS, Commonwealth of Australia

Bates, A W (1995) *Technology, Open Learning and Distance Education*, Routledge, London

Bates, A W (2000) *Managing Technological Change: Strategies for college and university leaders*, Jossey-Bass, Windsor, Ontario

Educational Technology and Society, Journal of the International Forum of Educational Technology & Society and the IEEE Learning Technology Task Force (http://ifets.ieee.org/periodical/)

Ehrmann, S C (1997) 'Asking the right question: What does research tell us about technology and higher learning?', Annenberg/CPD, Washington, DC (www.learner.org/edtech/rscheval/rightquestion.html)

Eisenstadt, M and Vincent, T (eds) (1998) *The Knowledge Web: Learning and collaborating on the Net*, Kogan Page, London

Evans, T and Nation, D (eds) (2000) *Changing University Teaching: Reflections on creating educational technologies*, Kogan Page, London

Gilbert, S W (2000) 'A new vision worth working toward – Connected education and collaborative change', The TLT Group, The American Association for Higher Education, (www.tltgroup.org/gilbert/NewVwwt2000-2-14-00.htm)

Harasim, L (1989) 'On-line education: A new domain', in R Mason and A Kaye (eds), *Mindweave: Communication, computers and distance education*, pp 50–57, Pergamon Press, Oxford (www-icdl.open.ac.uk/mindweave/mindweave.html)

Harasim, L, Hiltz, S R, Teles, L and Turoff, M (1995) *Learning Networks: A field guide to teaching and learning on-line*, MIT Press, Cambridge, MA

Horton, W (2000) *Designing Web-based Training*, Wiley, New York

International Journal of Educational Technology (www.outreach.uiuc.edu/ijet/)

Jonassen, D H, Peck, K L, Wilson, B G and Pfeiffer, W S (1998) *Learning with Technology: A constructivist perspective*, Prentice Hall, New Jersey

Journal of Asynchronous Learning Networks (www.aln.org/alnweb/journal/jaln.htm)

Katz, R N (ed) (1999) *Dancing with the Devil : Information technology and the new competition in higher education*, Jossey-Bass, San Francisco, CA

Kaye, A R (ed) (1992) *Collaborative Learning through Computer Conferencing: The Najaden papers*, Springer-Verlag, London

Khan, B H (ed) (1997) *Web-based Instruction*, Educational Technology Publications, Englewood Cliffs, NJ

Laurillard, D (1993) *Rethinking University Teaching: A framework for the effective use of educational technology*, Routledge, London

Paloff, R M and Pratt, K (1999) *Building Learning Communities in Cyberspace: Effective strategies for the online classroom*, Jossey-Bass, San Francisco, CA

Paloff, R M and Pratt, K (2000) *Lessons from the Cyberspace Classroom: Realities of online teaching*, Jossey-Bass, San Francisco, CA

Roblyer, M D and Edwards, J (2000) *Multimedia Edition of Integrating Educational Technology into Teaching*, Prentice Hall, New Jersey

Salmon, G (2000) *E-moderating: The key to teaching and learning online*, Kogan Page, London

Sanders, W B (2000) *Creating Learning-centered Courses for the World Wide Web*, Allyn & Bacon, Needham Heights, MA

Index

access 106, 155, 156
activity-based approach 115, 116
assessment 51, 58, 60, 65, 66, 71–74,
    102, 104, 157, 159, 172
  authentic 45
  criteria 76–78
  negotiation 78
  'over-correcting' 38
Authorware 123, 127, 132

bulletin board 82

case accounts/methods 7
case study 3, 4, 174
  benefits 7
  questions 6
Central Queensland University 91
classroom 2
collaboration 36, 39, 40–42, 52, 74,
    77, 79, 164, 171, 173
  collaborative learning environments
    5, 37, 73, 115, 116, 133
community building 43
compassionate pioneers 168, 169
computer-mediated communication
    (CMC) 78, 152
conflict 13, 173
  intervention 18
  resolution 49, 50
constructivist approaches 79
course/project team 99, 100–102, 122
crashing 92

Deakin University 146

debate 17–20, 56, 57, 59, 66–70, 74,
    75, 76, 77, 92
dialogue 33, 34
discussion forum/group 24, 37,
    39–42, 55–57, 63, 115
  incentives 67
  participation 64, 65
distance education 21, 99, 100, 105,
    146, 152

early adopters 1, 168, 169
e-mail 44, 63, 66, 75, 105, 118, 156
evaluation 41, 68, 97, 100, 118, 122,
    123, 125, 132, 133, 151, 157, 161,
    172
experiential learning environment 45

feedback 17, 39, 70, 85, 87, 96, 103,
    118, 157, 172
FirstClass 142, 151
flame war 15, 18
flexibility/flexible learning 56, 115,
    155, 162

Hong Kong 13
Hong Kong Institute of Education
    129
'hui' 28–35

information and communication
    technology (ICT) 127, 139–45,
    159
information technology (IT) 2, 104,
    129, 130

innovation   85–87, 120, 122, 162, 167, 168, 172, 174
instructional management system (IMS) 153, 166
interaction   5, 14, 21, 22–25, 35, 45, 51, 52, 55–59, 68, 82, 95, 115, 119, 120, 152, 172
InterLearn   34, 117, 118

learner demographics   24
learning organizations   167
learning outcomes   86
learning styles   133
lexicon   124
lifelong learning   30, 167
links   82, 83
listserv   32, 44–51,
lurkers   57, 77

mailbombing   15, 17
maintenance   112
moderator/s   46, 47, 49, 51, 52, 96, 172, 173
Monash University   34, 114, 118
monitor   85
multimedia   130–32, 134, 139
multiple-choice questions   60

negotiation   85, 98
netiquette   15
newsgroups   13
nicknames   14, 19

online learning   1, 3, 85, 86, 114, 117, 147, 152, 165
  issues   5
  participation   39, 40, 69, 87

passive students   18

planning   171
portal   165
postings   29
PowerPoint   56, 60
problem-based learning   160, 163, 164

ranting   30
reflection   6, 7, 49, 50, 77, 86, 97, 148, 161

scenario planning   93
searching   84
simulation   163, 164
software/courseware development   116–19, 121, 122, 124, 163
staff development and training   107–113, 119, 120, 146, 153, 173
student-centred learning   55, 60, 86
Student Network   22–24

teamwork   47, 48, 171
templates   111
threading/thread-mapping   35, 40, 59
tutorials   63, 93
tutors   100

University of Auckland   28
University of British Columbia   28
University of East Anglia   107
University of New Mexico   36
University of the South Pacific   99, 106
University of Warwick   139

videoconferencing   91, 95, 97, 105, 174
virtual classroom/learning   79, 160, 164
visual literacy   130, 135

Other titles in the 'Case Studies of Teaching in Higher Education' series:

Lecturing: Case studies, experience and practice edited by Helen Edwards, Brenda Smith and Graham Webb
This book brings together the guidance and advice of experienced lecturers and will be invaluable for all readers seeking to develop or refresh their lecturing, whatever their subject area or level of experience.

Problem-Based Learning: Case studies, experience and practice edited by Peter Schwartz, Stewart Mennin and Graham Webb
Offering compelling insights into the methods, challenges, applications and experiences of teaching with PBL, this book is for those currently using PBL as well as those new to it.